Martha Freud

Martha and Sigmund Freud
Silver Wedding Anniversary, 1911, in Klobenstein in South Tyrol

Martha Freud

A Biography

ℓ

KATJA BEHLING

Translated by R. D. V. Glasgow

polity

First published in German as *Martha Freud: die Frau des Genies*
© Aufbau Taschenbuch Verlag

This translation first published in 2005 © Polity Press

The right of Katja Behling to be identified as Author of this Work has been asserted
in accordance with the UK Copyright, Designs and Patents Act 1988.

First published in 2005 by Polity Press

Polity Press
65 Bridge Street
Cambridge CB2 1UR, UK

Polity Press
350 Main Street
Malden, MA 02148, USA

ISBN: 0-7456-3338-2

A catalogue record for this book is available from the British Library.

Text design by Peter Ducker
Typeset in Adobe Sabon 10.25 on 13pt
by Servis Filmsetting Ltd, Manchester
Printed and bound in Great Britain by
TJ International Ltd, Padstow, Cornwall

For further information on Polity, visit our website: www.polity.co.uk

Contents

Contents

Illustrations

The Freud Museum in London was kind enough to make the Bernays-Freud photographs available to us. For the photographs of Hamburg and Wandsbek we should like to thank Jens Wunderlich, Hamburg, and for the pictures of the Schloss Tegel sanatorium our thanks go to Ulrich and Christine von Heinz, Berlin.

Foreword by Anton W. Freud

Biographers of Sigmund Freud – and there are many of them – have tended to belittle, if not ignore, the part played in the development of psychoanalysis by Martha Freud, who stood by him in marriage for fifty-three years. After all, it is often said, she was just the wife, the one who looked after the house and children. Yet from my own experience I know such a point of view to be completely wrong. The author is to be thanked for conveying a different picture of how things were.

Martha was born in Hamburg, where she spent the formative early years of her life before moving to Vienna. Her grandfather was the chief rabbi of Hamburg, and her family had connections with many of the city's most prominent Jews, including the Warburgs and the Heines. Her North German upbringing had made her immune, so to speak, to any form of shoddiness or sloppiness, any temptation to botch a job or leave it half done. Martha was from a tougher, more disciplined school. Everything had to be just right. Jobs were to be done properly and punctually. There was no place for unruly or slovenly behaviour in the Freud household.

Martha's first child was born thirteen months after the wedding, a total of six children making their appearance within the next eight years. The strain of this alone could have ended in chaos. Far from it. Not only were there a host of mouths to be fed, but Sigmund still had to establish himself in his profession, for a doctor's income was directly dependent upon the number of patients he had. If Martha had not been willing or able to take on the burden herself, it would have been Sigmund who had to change the nappies, prepare the meals and look after the hordes of children. My father, Martin Freud, once told me, probably exaggerating slightly, that he could not remember a single time when at least one of the six children was not ill or infirm. At Berggasse 19 the Freuds had a large twelve-room apartment with eleven people living in it: the parents, Martha's sister Minna, six children, and at least two servants. Life had to be organized, the food provided, the stoves kept alight in winter, the young children taken to school and suchlike, and clothes – along with all the other things a family might need – had to be bought.

For all his other skills, Sigmund was to the best of my knowledge neither handy nor practically minded. I never saw him holding any work tool other than his fountain pen, and I have my serious doubts as to whether he could have knocked a nail into the wall to hang up a picture. The daily grind was organized, delegated and in part also carried out by Martha so her husband could devote himself entirely to his vocation. And this he certainly did, seeing patients from morning to evening, giving lectures, and at night writing his books. No one could be more justified than he was in quoting Kipling's poem 'If': 'If you can fill the unforgiving minute / With sixty seconds' worth of distance run – / Yours is the Earth and everything that's in it.' Freud wrote *The Interpretation of Dreams*, the book that meant most to him, between 1895 and 1899. In 1895 his eldest daughter was eight, and his eldest son six. Would he have had the time and opportunity to write this foundational work if he had had, say, to take his daughter to her dancing classes and his son to his riding lessons twice a week? Such commitment to family affairs was not expected at the time. His youngest daughter was born in 1895. When she cried in the night, was it Sigmund who got up to comfort her? Martha had assumed all these responsibilities so that Sigmund would have his peace of mind and enough time undisturbed to develop and articulate his thoughts. If Martha had been less efficient or unwilling to devote her life to her husband in this way, the flow of Sigmund's early ideas would have dried to a trickle before they could converge into a great sea. Martha always saw to it that her husband's energies were not squandered. Yet this is only half the story. On top of this, she herself exerted an influence – in particular through her personality and her relationship to Sigmund – upon the delicate bud of psychoanalysis, allowing it to grow and flourish. Few people in his life had so great an influence upon him. The aim of the following account is to show what sort of a person she was, to portray her character and trace the life she led. Using the relevant literature, correspondence and diaries, the author describes the person Martha Freud and the vital role played by *Frau Professor* in the life and work of her husband.

Oxted/London, July 2002

Preface

Countless books have been written about Sigmund Freud, dealing with both his life and his work. Married to him for over half a century, Martha Freud leaves her mark to varying degrees in these books. Her life takes shape only in relation to his. Although the literature contains many articles about Martha as a person, she has not so far had a biography dedicated to her. The present portrait cannot hope to be exhaustive either, since essential sources will not be available for years to come. Yet the woman at Freud's side has provided a wealth of material for fictional scenarios. This speaks of the great interest she arouses and at the same time illustrates how little is still basically known about her.

Nearly all of these fictions turn on the image of Martha as an irreproachable bourgeois wife. They elaborate a plot that hinges on the question 'What if . . . ?' What would have happened if Martha had been much less puritanical than she is generally assumed to have been? Françoise Xenakis (1986) takes up this theme and portrays Martha as a woman both virtuous and sophisticated, a woman who harbours secret fantasies and shows her husband the way towards female sexuality by laying the groundwork for theories that relate to these fantasies. The French authors Laurence Paton and Lisa Llobregat (1989) have written Martha's diaries, painting the picture of a woman who loves her husband and sees the sacrifices demanded of her in the same light as the discipline and persistent tenacity characteristic of her husband. Nonetheless, the occasional wistful sigh can be heard to escape from their Martha, and it is with the help of a certain amount of *poudre magique* that she copes with their endlessly long engagement, cocaine giving her both the strength to cope and the rosy cheeks Sigmund is so fond of. In his epic *The Passions of the Mind*

(1971), Irving Stone portrays Martha as a person whose opinion is important to Sigmund Freud and whose influence on him is considerable. In the play *Berggasse 19* (1979) by Henry Denker, Martha functions in a similar capacity as the woman at Freud's side.

In one of the three apocalyptic stories making up *The End of the World News* (1983), Anthony Burgess's Martha trenchantly deflates psychoanalysis with a succinct assessment of her husband's commitment as she passes her friend a cup of coffee: 'If it's not one thing it's another. First it's Oedipus. Now it's dreams.' C. G. Jung's wife takes the same line: 'Oh, Carl's always seeing this. The occult, he calls it.' Jean-Paul Sartre's *The Freud Scenario* (1985), originally written in 1958, on which director John Huston based his 1961 film *Freud, the Secret Passion*, highlights Martha's independence and the spirit of opposition with which she teases her fiancé, also tracing the changes in their relationship over the years. In the novel *Henry James' Midnight Song* (1993) by Carol de Chellis-Hill, Martha bewitches an officer who is called to the Berggasse to solve a murder mystery. In the hands of Fotini Tsalikoglou (2000), the first-person narrator, supposedly Martha Freud, turns out to be an unidentified woman prey to forbidden, shameless thoughts, dark longings and secret desires. The Canadian writer Hélène Richard (1993) paints a fanciful picture of Martha as a caring analyst's wife, who also plays an important role for the patients and engages their fantasies.

In the feature film *The Seven-Per-Cent Solution* (1976), the great English detective Sherlock Holmes is a guest of the Freuds in turn-of-the-century Vienna, eating and conversing at table with Sigmund and Martha. The idea, engineered by Holmes's loyal assistant Dr Watson, is that the neurologist should cure the sleuth's cocaine addiction, which in the end is what happens. Before this comes about, however, Sherlock Holmes must pass through the torments of cold turkey in the rooms of Berggasse 19, where he finds himself day and night in the grip of fearsome fantasies and hallucinations. When Martha brings the exhausted patient a bowl of soup to his bedside, instead of soup all Holmes sees is a revolting mass of wriggling worms, prompting him to knock the bowl from her hands in horror. Jumping up in confusion, Holmes now sees his entire bed teeming with snakes and insects. Even Martha's cheeks have something crawling across them. For a matter of seconds her rigid face takes on an air of sadistic cruelty, as though she and her husband – and possibly others – were caught up in dark conspiracy against him. The grotesquery of the film would have perhaps amused Martha's husband. After all, he was a keen reader of the Sherlock Holmes novels written by his 'colleague', the former doctor Sir Arthur Conan Doyle.

The question is whether Martha Freud would have recognized herself in any of these made-up tales. She was certainly not one to seek out the limelight: she was happy with a place in the background, although she did enjoy her position as *Frau Professor* at the side of her world-famous husband. She was keen not to cause controversy herself, and she never said or did the wrong thing. In her eyes reserve and decency were among the highest virtues. Yet Martha also exerted an enormous influence on the emergence of psychoanalysis. She set the course for her husband to follow in the production of his life's work, provided material for his writings, and as a wife provided the conditions that would allow him to rise up to join the ranks of intellectual greats. Many wives of the time saw their vocation as being to support their husbands' advancement as best they could. Martha's individual fate in this sense represents the fate of many of her contemporaries. This goes especially for her experiences as a German Jew. Here too her life stands for countless other dramatic life-stories from the time between the end of the nineteenth century and National Socialism. For Martha Freud herself, however, her biography is likely to have been above all a timeless story of extraordinary love and loyal affection.

K. B.

Acknowledgements

The author would like to thank all those who have contributed to the writing of this book. Special thanks go to Anton W. Freud, who devoted considerable time and support to the project. Thanks also go to Michael Molnar of the Freud Museum, London, Thomas Roberts and Mark Paterson of Sigmund Freud Copyrights, the staff of the State Archives of Hamburg, as well as Magdalena Frank of the Aufbau publishing house.

The translator would like to thank the staff at the Freud Museum, London, for their kind assistance.

Hamburg, Bei den Hütten, about 1900
This is where Martha Bernays was born, on 26 July 1861

℘

Hamburg

A Hamburg Childhood

Martha Bernays, Freud's future sweetheart and wife, was born on 26 July 1861 in the Protestant city of Hamburg. She was the daughter of the merchant Berman Bernays and his wife Emmeline Philipp. The Philipps, a family of reputable traders, came from Sweden. The Bernays were one of the most highly regarded Jewish families in the city, counting some notable scholars in their midst. The father's name is said to have originally been 'Beer' or 'Behr'. After 1789, this was changed to its francophone variant in recognition of the improvements in the situation of Jews as a consequence of the French Revolution: the Jews of Hamburg were granted complete constitutional equality in 1860.[1] 'Bernays' echoed the original name as well as the French pronunciation of the village from which it stemmed, Bernay in the Seine Valley in Normandy.[2]

Over the generations the Bernays family had acquired respectability rather than wealth. Martha's parents could make ends meet, but the young girl was hardly born with a silver spoon in her mouth. Her earliest years were spent in what is now Neustadt, at Bei den Hütten no. 61,[3] a street that bordered on what was known as the 'Alley Quarter'. This jumbled maze of narrow alleyways and backyards was inaccessible to vehicles and virtually impenetrable to daylight. It was inhabited by hordes of people, many of them Jews, who lived crowded closely together in often dilapidated half-timbered houses and wholly inadequate sanitary conditions. Cheap, close to the harbour, the Alley Quarter was viewed in better circles as a breeding ground for crime, prostitution and social disorder.[4] Around 1860 there was discussion of whether to pull the area down or redevelop it. Some time after

Martha's birth, speculators and leading civic figures took the matter into their own hands. The first step, in 1867, was to lay down the Wexstrasse as an attractive corridor running through its northern tip. Decades later, the new road was to play an agreeable part in the family history. It was here that the newly married Freuds laid on their wedding meal in 1886, at the Hotel Hirschel.

The modest circumstances in which they lived were not the only problem faced by Martha's parents Berman and Emmeline. Their son Isaac (1855–72) suffered from a severe hip disorder and needed crutches to walk. The couple had a total of seven children, born in quick succession, three of whom, Fabian, Michael and Sara, died in babyhood between August 1857 and April 1859.[5] Child mortality was common at the time, and a large number of offspring could be a burden, but the loss of several children one after the other must have come as a severe blow to Martha's parents and left them insecure as to the fate of the others.

February 1860 saw the birth of Elias, known to everyone as Eli. It was with him, Isaac and Minna, four years her junior, that Martha Bernays grew up. She was devoted to her elder brothers, and her sister remained very close to her throughout her life. Isaac, in a special position anyway on account of his handicap, was his mother's favourite. Throughout the period when she was losing one child after another, he remained her only son. Her second boy, Eli, was generally treated 'rather harshly' by Emmeline.[6] This imbalance naturally kindled the rivalry of the two brothers.

The situation changed abruptly when Isaac died in 1872. His death was a heavy blow to his mother in particular, as well as to Martha, who henceforth grew even closer to Eli and Minna. Eli was now the only son in the family and felt the full force of his mother's grief. His role changed once again seven years later when his father died and he became the breadwinner and head of the family. Yet Emmeline had no intention of leaving the running of the household entirely in Eli's hands. Having lost one of their parents, the minors needed a legal guardian, and a widowed woman found herself in a different social position from a man in similar circumstances. Yet there were certain matters where she stood her ground and insisted on her rights. This led to conflicts with Eli, although her son generally knew how to find a solution that would keep them both happy. Their relationship was never especially close, yet Eli always complied with his 'duties as a son' and was very fond of his sisters. He did everything he could to help Martha in particular.[7]

Martha's birth in 1861 seems to have fallen in a period of financial hardship, with the family at the time unable to meet its commitments towards Hamburg's German-Israeli community.[8] Tax arrears with the Jewish community might also have been the reason that the children were not entered in the birth register until years later, probably from Vienna in 1880 and in connection with inheritance certificates issued following the death of their father.[9] Despite the father's greatest efforts, their financial straits became increasingly critical. He had originally run a 'linen and embroidery shop' at Alter Wall 2, on the corner with Schleusenbrücke,[10] but on giving up this business in 1860 he moved to the advertising firm Haasenstein & Vogler, a nationwide concern with its Hamburg office at Grosse Johannisstrasse 14. According to the contract dated 6 July 1860, Berman Bernays was entitled to 50 per cent of the revenue from the adverts he sold, which were above all for health resorts in central and southern Germany.[11] He was working on a commission basis, in other words, and the pay was relatively unpredictable. Perhaps it was because of the resulting fluctuations in income that Berman Bernays began to trade in securities. His family had quite a nose for business. At Neuer Wall 63, Martha's uncle, Louis Bernays, ran a 'stock of hairs, feathers and bristles',[12] and her father too seems for a while to have made considerable winnings in his wheeling and dealing. In 1865 – the year Minna was born – the family moved to a flat in the Mühlenstrasse,[13] where they employed two servants and were now able to pay back what they owed in annual taxes.[14]

Following the death of three children and a period of financial turbulence, from 1860 – when Eli was born and their father's professional career took a new turn – things appeared for a while to pick up again both financially and privately. Unfortunately, the lucky streak did not last long. Bernays had got involved in shady business in stocks and shares that was to be his undoing. Early in December 1867 financial ruin caught up with him, and he was arrested,[15] and on 5 December 1867 the 42-year-old Bernays was

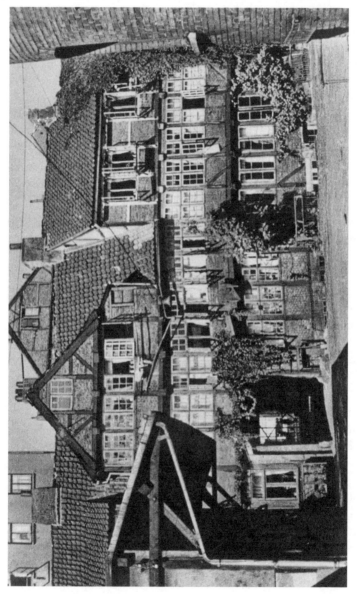

Hamburg, Mühlenstrasse, about 1935
The Bernays family moved into this street in 1865

declared bankrupt before Hamburg Commercial Court.[16] The net result of his ill-advised speculation was debts of some 60,000 German marks. Complex insolvency proceedings were instigated. The receivers established that no accounts had been kept of income and expenditure, while the bankrupt Bernays himself was unable to provide precise information about what had become of the individual sums of money or how much he owed to whom.[17] Painstakingly, casual notes and other evidence of his liabilities and business activities were assembled, page upon page of records drawn up, creditors registered, and calculations made of debits and credits. An inventory recorded his possessions from furniture, gold jewellery and net curtains right through to the very last watering can. Despite having broken the law, Bernays was subsequently released and granted freedom of movement to pursue his business ventures. This concession, which was to ensure that his family was provided for, meant that with the permission of the courts, the police and his creditors he was allowed to make journeys to central Germany to canvass for business on behalf of Haasenstein & Vogler.[18] On 15 June 1868 he was sentenced to one year's prison for fraudulent bankruptcy, and in October of the same year he began to serve his sentence. As a result of several petitions made to the Senate of the Free Hanseatic City of Hamburg, he was released on 30 July 1869.

The Move to Vienna

On his release from prison, Bernays accepted gratefully when his old company offered him a job in Vienna at their branch at Wollzeile no. 9.[19] The son of a high-ranking rabbi, he could count on his contacts to make a new start possible for him far from Hamburg. They did not let him down. Conveniently, this solution meant that no further shadow was cast on the reputation of family or firm, and a scandal could be avoided. Of course, there were those who claimed the whole affair was just an elegant pretext for unobtrusively spiriting away a young reprobate. Yet among the court records a letter from the firm to Berman Bernays suggests that his superiors continued to place their trust in him: after all, he was not a serious offender. They regarded him as a capable worker and, as the document put it, wanted to accommodate him on the basis of their good cooperation in the past. Unfortunately, the letter explained, as a result of his 'imprisonment' they had had to fill his position in Hamburg, and so it was only possible to offer him a vacant post in Vienna.[20]

In 1869, when Martha was eight, the family moved to Vienna. For as long as she lived, Martha never forgot her mother's sorrow at leaving Hamburg and the sizzling of her tears as they landed on the hot cooking stove.[21] Even so, things started well, and their situation became more stable. The respected family from Hamburg was assimilated into its new neighbourhood and quickly established social contacts. Berman Bernays was soon able to improve his position, accepting what was presumably a more lucrative post as secretary to the well-known political economist, constitutional law expert, and university professor Lorenz von Stein. As a consequence of this change of profession, when Martha and Sigmund Freud married in 1886 the profession of the bride's father was given as 'journalist',[22] whereas in Hamburg he had always been a 'merchant'.

After a while Martha settled down, made friends, and did her best to adapt to her new circumstances. This included confronting what to her ears was the unfamiliar Austrian dialect. Although she was always credited with speaking faultless German, following the move she is said to have gradually lost her marked North German accent – to the express disapproval of her father – and moved closer to her new surroundings in the way she spoke. At the outset, however, Martha's classmates had apparently believed that certain peculiarities of her Hamburg diction – especially her characteristic pronunciation of 'st' and 'sp' at the beginning of a word – were some sort of defect or disorder, and teased the newcomer about her accent.[23]

In 1872, when Martha was eleven, her brother Isaac died at the age of sixteen. The loss of a brother was something she shared with her future husband, who experienced the same thing in early childhood. An unconscious desire to compensate for the loss they had suffered may thus have played a part when Sigmund and Martha as well as his sister and her brother later married one another: the cross-weaving of in-laws was perhaps a psychological attempt to win back the siblings they had lost.[24]

Seven years after the death of her brother there followed the unexpected demise of Martha's father when, on the cold night of 9 December 1879, Berman Bernays suddenly collapsed and died in the street as a consequence of 'heart failure'. The death certificate recorded that the 'editor, 53 years of age, Mosaic by birth', had died of 'paralysis of the heart'; his place of residence and of death, Rembrandtgasse no. 3, Vienna [District] II.[25] Bernays had lived to see the end of his insolvency proceedings. The files give 23 January 1873 as the date of exoneration.[26]

Even so, Berman Bernays left virtually no legacy. After his death, it was his brothers and sisters who supported the family, while nineteen-year-old Eli also contributed to their upkeep, taking over his father's post as secretary. The widow established temporary guardians for the children who had not yet come of age. These included the father of Bertha Pappenheim,[27] the woman who under the name of Anna O. later went down as the first patient in the history of psychoanalysis. Von Stein too, long since a friend of the family, as well as lawyers and of course the elder brother acted as legal representatives of the wards Minna and Martha.[28]

Even in her Vienna years, Martha kept up contact with the city of her infancy. Hamburg was the indisputable focal point of two decisive phases in her life, her early childhood and her years of engagement. Throughout her life she remained at heart a patriotic citizen of Hamburg, almost matching her mother in her attachment to their home city. Neither she nor Minna ever made the slightest concession to the spirit or lifestyle of Vienna, and even after fifty years in Austria they still spoke perfect standard German. As a result Martha always came across as rather exotic in Vienna. She exuded something of an aura of worldliness, which contributed to the special atmosphere of the house: her exotic quality reinforced the impression visitors to the Berggasse had of immersion in a weirdly 'extraterritorial' realm.[29]

Martha was always glad of any occasion that might take her to Hamburg, and in subsequent stages of her life there continued to be plenty of these. Flying visits to relatives and trips to look after her ailing mother repeatedly brought her back to her home city. On 18 January 1913, her daughter Sophie married a distant relative,[30] the well-known Hamburg portrait photographer

Martha Bernays, about 1872

Max Halberstadt. Max was a 'chivalrous-looking'[31] man from a middle-class background, with 'no wealth, no high rank, which is all the same to us too', as Freud wrote on 20 July 1912.[32] Like the Bernays, the Halberstadts were related to a famous rabbi family, the Carlebachs.[33]

Max Halberstadt had a studio at Neuer Wall no. 54, and from time to time published his work in the photographic journal *Photofreund*, which in 1927 dedicated a special edition to his works.[34] Yet his studio did not always fare well, and there were occasions when he needed the support of his celebrated father-in-law.[35] In March 1914 the young couple's first son was born. Sophie and her son spent periods of the war in Vienna, living there between January 1916 and 15 May 1917. After staying just over a week at the Pension Hoofe, An der Alster no. 18, in Hamburg,[36] she then moved on to Schwerin, where Martha visited her under difficult conditions.[37] In this city, where Sophie's husband had contacts, her second son was born in 1918. Not until 27 March 1919 was she 'back with her husband',[38] as substantiated by documents such as her 'bread coupon cancellation form'.[39] Less than a year later, on 25 January 1920 and in the early stages of her third pregnancy,[40] Sophie suddenly died of severe influenza. She was buried in the Jewish cemetery of Hamburg-Ohlsdorf in the most difficult of circumstances: the country was in turmoil; there were virtually no trains running; her parents were unable to attend. Only Ernst and Oliver managed to get to Hamburg from Berlin to take part in the funeral. 'It seems to have been a very dignified and impressive ceremony', wrote Freud.[41]

Sophie Freud and Max Halberstadt had two sons: Wolfgang Ernst Halberstadt, born in 1914 and known as Ernstl, who after the death of his father adopted his mother's maiden name, and his brother Heinz, known as Heinerle,[42] who died in 1923 at the age of four and a half. Ernst was a pupil at the *Simonschule* and the *Lichtwarkschule* in Hamburg.[43] Later he attended the private *Lehmann-Schule*, where his future stepmother Berta Katzenstein, Max Halberstadt's second wife, worked as a teacher.[44] The paths of the Hamburg Halberstadts and the Viennese Freuds took separate courses from 1936 onwards, when Max was forced for 'political-financial' reasons[45] to emigrate to South Africa, Freud helping him by providing him with contacts.[46] Max Halberstadt died in Johannesburg in December 1940.

Isaac Bernays, Martha's Grandfather

Isaac ben Jacob Bernays (1792–1849), a native of Mainz, was a well-known rabbi.[47] The influence he exerted provides a key to the self-image of the Bernays family, which in turn explains certain conflicts in the relationship between Martha and Sigmund, specifically in the matter of religion.

From his early years Isaac Bernays had a reputation as a child prodigy, staggering those around him with his feats in religious studies.[48] He was one of the first Jewish 'guest' students to attend Würzburg University.[49] After completing his studies in Würzburg, where he was a student of the well-known Talmudist R. Abraham Bing among others, he went to Munich to work as a private tutor in the household of a certain Herr von Hirsch.[50] Here too Bernays made use of the broad range of academic possibilities without setting any store by a formal degree to complete his scholarly studies.[51] Following this, he lived for a while as a private scholar in his native city of Mainz. Yet Bernays rapidly carved out a career for himself. By 1821 the German-Jewish community of Hamburg had appointed him as their leader. The young minister with the 'philosopher's face'[52] categorically declined the title of rabbi,[53] insisting instead on the Spanish-Jewish scholarly designation 'Chacham'. This signalled a new start in the spiritual care of his coreligionists.[54]

Once appointed by the community elders, Bernays turned his attention to the Talmud Torah charity school, founded in 1805, where the children had previously only been taught Hebrew and arithmetic.[55] In 1822 he initiated its reformation. Working with the school governors, he transformed the basic structure of the education it provided by adding subjects from public elementary schools – German, natural science, geography and history – to the traditional curriculum. At the same time he shifted the focus of the religious education to the study of the Bible.[56] By 1827, what had previously been just a class in religion had turned into a model primary school. This success was all the more noteworthy since compulsory school attendance for children was not introduced until the much later date of November 1870, when the Hamburg Senate enacted a law providing basic primary and secondary education for all children between the ages of six and fourteen in the subjects of religion, German language, arithmetic, geography, history, physics, chemistry, drawing, gym, English and where possible French, as well as needlework in girls' schools.[57]

Bernays did not meet only with acclaim and support in what he did. His religious reforms in particular met with the opposition of 'ascetic fanatics'.[58] Isaac Bernays, who spoke several languages, possessed a broad education, was well versed in philosophy and exceptionally well acquainted with the Bible, Midrash and Talmud, constantly sought to translate the traditional Jewish self-understanding into a more modern form without departing from the basic orthodoxy. He was the first German rabbi prepared to incorporate German into the service. This did not meet with universal approval either. His innovative sermons caused a considerable stir, yet for many Jews his convoluted sentence structures and complex trains of thought were impossible to follow.[59]

Despite his modernizing inclinations, Martha's grandfather was at the same time an opponent of certain religious reforms. What was important in his eyes was reflection on the essence of the faith. He made worshippers keep stricter discipline and order than was usual, wanting to create an atmosphere of deeper reverence.[60] When the Israelite Temple of Hamburg – a reform synagogue that had partially broken with established forms of Jewish worship – brought out its revised prayer book in 1841, it was Bernays who voiced the protest of the Jewish 'Old Believers', who still formed a clear majority but saw their position as threatened in the long term. Bernays committed himself fervently – though ultimately unsuccessfully – to countering the processes of pluralization and fragmentation among Jews.[61]

In his final years, things quietened down around Isaac Bernays. He continued to devote himself passionately to studying the Jewish philosophy of religion and also gave lectures, although as he did not keep a written record of his ideas the writings of the Chacham are virtually non-existent.[62] He died suddenly of apoplexy in 1849 and was buried in the Grindel Cemetery.[63] Heinrich Heine acknowledged him as an extraordinary personality. Isaac's brother, who edited the Jewish newspaper *Vorwärts* in Paris, was one of the first to publish a poem by Heine, and through him the poet once sent greetings to Karl Marx.[64] The ties between the Bernays family and the Heine family referred to by Martha's grandson Anton W. Freud in the foreword have their roots in this period, and go back to Martha's grandfather Isaac.

One year after taking office, Isaac Bernays had married eighteen-year-old Sara Lea Berend (1804–58) from Hanover, Martha's

Isaac Bernays
Martha's grandfather, chief rabbi of Hamburg

grandmother. Sara Lea Berend was the daughter of the Hanover court purveyor and businessman Michael Berend and his wife Rosalie Eger. Isaac and Sara Lea had nine children.[65] One of their daughters, Lea (1829–1924), whose married name was Löw-Beer (Löwbeer), later provided the financial support that made possible the long-awaited marriage between her niece Martha and Sigmund Freud. The sons Jacob (1824–81), Michael (1834–97) and Martha's father Berman (1826–79) were the best known of the nine children. Jacob and Michael both took up academic careers.

Professor Jacob Bernays, who died unmarried and childless and left his fortune to Martha and her brother and sister, made his mark as a classicist in Breslau, Bonn and Heidelberg.[66] The circles in which he moved included Paul Heyse, Georg Bunsen, Theodor Mommsen and others. Like his father, he was a man of strictly orthodox religious convictions, his Jewishness preventing him from taking on a regular professorship at Bonn University.

Michael Bernays started out studying law, before turning to literary history and making a name for himself as a Goethe and Shakespeare specialist. He was only fourteen when his father died. In 1856 he converted to Christianity and was baptized, a momentous step that on the one hand completely estranged him from his family[67] but on the other furthered his career. He became a highly respected and exceptionally prolific professor in Munich, counting among his friends King Ludwig II of Bavaria.

In their own ways, both Michael and Jacob cemented the reputation of the Bernays as a family of leading scholars. This was not unimportant to Sigmund Freud. His choice of wife was from the intellectual circles to which he himself aspired.[68]

Berman Bernays, Martha's Father

Unlike his famous brothers, Berman[69] did not take up an academic career but instead became a businessmen like his younger brother Louis,[70] albeit less successfully so.[71] It is difficult to shed much light on the relationship between father and daughter. Martha was always silent on the matter, and even members of the family found it hard to form an impression of Berman.[72] One reason for this reserve might be the insolvency episode, which turned the family life of the Bernays and the world of young Martha upside-down.

Little is known of the consequences of this episode within the family, of what the six-year-old girl was told, or what she inferred from the behaviour of her mother and other people. Her father had broken the law and been sent to prison. The man who always strove to set his family an example in moral and religious values – an impostor? Martha is said never to have talked about this blot on her father's copybook,[73] in itself a testimony to the gravity of the matter. Other members of the family as well, if they ever knew anything, said nothing. It was only a few years ago that certain descendants of the family learnt of their great-grandfather's misdeed. This chapter of the family history was passed over more or less in silence, outwardly at least.

The insolvency incident – if it came to light at all – seems to have done little to damage relations between the Bernays family and the Freud family. According to the account given by Klaus Theweleit, Sigmund regarded Martha's father as a more respectable merchant than his own father Jacob[74] and the Bernays clan, including Eli, as altogether more decent than – for example – his own elder brothers 'with their dubious deals in Manchester, who also take care of "the family" but do so probably with forged money and credit papers'.[75] In late 1865 and early 1866, Josef Freud, the brother of Freud's father, was indicted and sent to prison for trading in counterfeit roubles, a 'traumatic' calamity for the whole family,[76] and Freud's father Jacob (1815–96), who until late in life passed himself off as a wool-merchant, was likewise the subject of rumours. At any event it was never clear how he succeeded in supporting his large family in Vienna. Again and again he is said to have contrived hopeful plans and promising projects that in the end always came to nothing. There were certainly relatives who helped the family out. Rumour had it that Jacob worked as an agent for Jewish traders from outside Vienna, providing them with contacts – or even that he kept his family above water by trafficking in counterfeit money.[77] The only thing certain is that Jacob did not stand out for his initiative or business acumen.[78]

There is no evidence, however, that misdeeds such as Berman Bernays's were taken lightly. On the contrary, the whole episode was an embarrassment and a disgrace. Whether his involvement was due to an unfortunate lack of expertise and know-how or whether it was an intentional act of embezzlement, he could be faulted at the very least for the non-transparency of his business dealings. No matter how you looked at it, something had gone seriously wrong.

The signs are that Martha never got over her father's misdemeanour, instead declaring it taboo. Perhaps this was why she constantly strove to be so irreproachably honest and upright, and could hardly have been more conservative or law-abiding.[79] She learnt to be outwardly steadfast, loyal and dutiful even when her inner convictions were being put to severe tests. It is unclear

Berman and Isaac Bernays
Martha's father and her brother, who died in 1872 at the age of sixteen

whether she inwardly distanced herself from her father or loved him unconditionally. She is said to have greatly revered him. For her grandson Anton W. Freud, it is impossible to tell the quality of this relationship, and he cannot vouch that it was even a good one.[80]

Yet Martha seems to have found her version of the truth and formed the image of a father who was upright and possibly even heroic. A clue to her attitude may be found in an episode recorded in her son's memoirs. These describe a walk in the park one day during a period of frequent riots, when the children, together with their nursemaid, suddenly came upon a group of uniformed policemen leading between them a handful of dishevelled students. When the *Kinderfrau* Josefine told the children not to look, since anyone arrested by the police could only be a wicked criminal, Martha Freud immediately interrupted to contradict the nursemaid's words, explaining that it was quite possible for a man who had been arrested for political reasons to be perfectly decent and even of a noble cast of mind: he might be putting his life and liberty at risk for convictions he believed to be right.[81] This was a remarkably liberal viewpoint. Perhaps her words were a way, in her mind, of coming to the aid of her father, or perhaps she was thinking of her husband. Either way, Martha proved herself to be a granddaughter worthy of her grandfather, as well as her mother's daughter. For her mother was not one to fight shy of obstacles either.

Emmeline Bernays, Martha's Mother

After a remarkable nine years of engagement, Berman Isaac Bernays in 1854 married Egla Philipp (1830–1910), who was known as Emmeline. Like Martha, therefore, Emmeline knew only too well about waiting years and years for the marriage she had set her heart on.

Emmeline was the daughter of the Hamburg merchant Fabian Aaron Philipp (1790–1850) and his wife Minna (1795–1861), née Ruben. Martha's grandfather Fabian Philipp came from Karlskrona in Sweden. His wife was born in Hamburg.[82] No details are known about Fabian Philipp's parents, Aaron Isaac Philipp and Ester Israel Polack, or about the circumstances that brought the Philipps from Sweden to Hamburg.

Emmeline had two brothers. One of them, Isaac (1827–44), died young, long before Martha was born. The other, Elias (1824–98), lived in Wandsbek near Hamburg at Claudiusstrasse no. 3,[83] where Martha used to spend her summers before her move back from Vienna to Hamburg in 1883. Uncle Elias was the witness when Martha and Sigmund accepted each other in marriage. He married twice, both marriages producing children. From the first marriage, to Clara Lewisohn (1830–72), came Fabian, Arnold, Fanny, Rudolf, Minna, Raphael and John, born between 1852 and 1865. This growing horde of cousins formed part of the circle of people that surrounded Martha during her years in Hamburg and Wandsbek and whom she occasionally mentioned in her letters to Sigmund. By the time of their wedding, Elias had already married Mary Heine, a native of Hamburg-Altona.[84] Elias and Mary had four children together: Julius, Egla-Elsa, Martha and Isaac-Oscar, born between 1878 and 1887.[85]

Emmeline was a practising orthodox Jew. The traditional *scheitel* was something she accepted as a matter of course, shaving her head for the celebration of her wedding and from then on wearing hairpieces.[86] Yet what she lacked in hair she is said to have made up for in hard-headedness. Outwardly Emmeline came over as 'mild, soft and angelically sweet',[87] yet this was deceptive. She always fought to have her own way, displaying a tenacity she knew how to turn to account. Freud did not care for this quality; after all, she used her weapons against him as well: 'I seek for similarities with you, but find hardly any', he wrote to Martha, describing his future mother-in-law as 'alien' to him. He found her arrogant and smug. 'Her very warm-heartedness has an air of condescension, and she exacts admiration', he claimed not long after becoming more closely acquainted with her.[88] He was also bothered by her desire to avoid unpleasantness at all costs, even if this meant resorting to evasions and deceptions.[89] What he liked least about her was that she did not selflessly put her children's interests first, as he was used to from his own adoring mother Amalie (1835–1930). As a widow Emmeline insisted on remaining head of the household and refused to budge an inch in this respect, which was something Freud greatly resented. He was confirmed in his view by his friend and fellow-sufferer Ignaz Schönberg, who intended to marry Emmeline's daughter Minna and was likewise starting to have his doubts about the mother. The two prospective sons-in-law were in complete agreement on the matter: in their eyes, Emmeline's position was pure selfishness.[90]

What is certain is that Martha found it difficult to break free from her dominant mother. Their special closeness can be explained by the personality of the two women, the family setting, and the upheavals in Martha's childhood, as well as maternal and social expectations. Emmeline Bernays was seen as a domineering

Emmeline Bernays
Martha's mother

woman, who had repeatedly in life had to confront situations that called upon her strength of character and forcefulness. For her more mild-mannered daughter it was not easy to face up to her mother in the same way. She preferred to avoid conflicts, and this led to discrepancies that sparked not a few conflicts during her years of engagement.

Emmeline found a considerably tougher opponent in her future son-in-law, whose mother was also a strong figure. Though less despotic than Amalie Freud, Emmeline was certainly regarded within the family as the sort of woman who would never yield to any sort of pressure. Freud once described her in the following terms: 'I see her as a person of great mental and moral power standing in our midst, capable of high accomplishments, without a trace of the absurd weaknesses of old women.' At the same time, however, there was no denying that she was taking 'a line against us all, like an old man'.[91] Martin Freud always remembered one incident involving his German grandmother that provides a particular illustration of her character. One day, when the whole family was out taking a stroll, they were caught in a sudden torrential downpour. In accordance with the principle of 'old people and children first', Sigmund and Martha Freud bundled Emmeline and a handful of children into the only available carriage and sent them home, packed like sardines into the small one-horse conveyance. Before long, the air in the overcrowded carriage was scarce to the point of asphyxiation. The children begged to be allowed to open the windows, yet Grandma Emmeline refused to let them on account of the rain. There immediately ensued a battle of willpower between a horde of headstrong children struggling for breath and a frail old lady resisting them. The frail old lady won hands down. The windows stayed closed.[92]

The Lovely Martha

Martha had a sheltered childhood in Hamburg and Vienna. The 'Prussian' virtues of decency, reliability, moral probity and perfectionism formed the ethos to be emulated, and in this respect Martha was seen as very 'German'.[93] Her parents, moreover, set great store by religious orthodoxy and imparted ideals such as family unity, modesty and restraint, self-sacrifice, faith in God, and devotion to a higher goal. After receiving a normal upbringing for a young (Jewish) girl from her background, attending the appropriate schools, Martha had a great thirst for knowledge and a special interest in art and literature, which Freud recognized and appreciated as soon as he met her. He found her his equal in discussing music. They read and talked about the same books, exchanging views, for example, on John Stuart Mill, whose works Freud translated, and Georg Brandes.[94] His first present to her was *David Copperfield*, a novel based closely on the life of its author Charles Dickens, which not only portrayed the struggle of a boy left to fend for himself in poverty but also featured an impecunious father figure (Mr Micawber) sent to prison for debt.[95] Dickens was one of Martha's favourite authors. She often referred to him in conversation and in January 1884 compared the hospital where her fiancé worked with the workers' 'fairy palaces' in Dickens's *Hard Times*. Some time later Sigmund warmly recommended she read Cervantes' *Don Quixote*, a book that made him laugh out loud. Only afterwards did it occur to him that it also contained a lot of rude parts and that 'the many coarse and in themselves nauseating passages' in it were 'no reading matter for girls'.[96] She read it anyway. Although as a girl of her time she never took up a career, even after she had left school she did all she could to broaden her horizons through cultural activities and the company she kept. It was above all her sharp mind that made her so attractive in her fiancé's eyes.

She was a distinctive, graceful figure with a feeling for style and her own characteristic charisma. Photos from these years show a petite figure with fine features, a clear expression and a harmonious profile. Her dark hair, parted down the middle, was worn in a plain style or up in a bun. She dressed tastefully and in a very feminine manner. In accordance with the fashion of the times, she had a preference for high-necked, close-fitting, long dresses in mainly muted colours, without gaudy patterns but elaborately decorated with tassels, tucks and pleats. The overall impression of elegance in the way she dressed was rounded off with lace-up ankle boots and a suitable hat. Martha and her husband-to-be thus made rather a smart couple, both of them setting store by their stylishness. This did not necessarily mean wearing jewellery. Some treasures, however, were so fashionable and sought-after at the time that even Freud was set on giving Martha a gold 'snake bangle'. As comments by Freud imply, this much-coveted piece of jewellery was also an exclusive status symbol worn by the elegant wives of *Privatdozente*, and it grieved him that for the time being she had to make do with a 'small silver snake'. Sigmund wanted to see her in the most beautiful attire so it would 'never occur to a soul that she could have married anyone but a prince'.[97]

Many men were attracted by young Martha's charms, and she had many suitors. One of these admirers was a certain Dr Steigenberger, who in 1884 was to work under Freud as an *Aspirant* or clinical assistant in the hospital and looked up to his victorious rival 'with awe'.[98] Martha had already turned down at least one proposal of marriage and was more than likely to receive others.[99] Later in life she described how before she met Sigmund she had almost got engaged to a much older businessman, Hugo Kadisch. Yet Eli had realized that she did not really love him and advised her against pursuing the match. For the rest of her life she was grateful to her brother for this piece of guidance.[100]

Kadisch was not to be the only contender. Within a week of their engagement Freud believed he had reason to be jealous. He had learnt that Martha was not only on close terms with one of her Hamburg cousins, the composer Max Mayer, but also found some of his songs deeply moving. An anxious Freud promptly demanded that she should not call her cousin familiarly by his first name, but use his surname.[101] Artists, Freud feared, posed a particular threat, for they had the means of effortlessly winning women over, while for scientists like himself this involved a laborious struggle. If the power of enchantment was further combined with love, as Freud suspected it was in the case of Max Mayer, the scientist's was a hopelessly lost cause. In his case, Freud himself admitted, this was exacerbated by a certain inexperience in his dealings with the opposite sex. He had not taken enough interest in women in his youth, and he was now paying the price.[102]

Freud sensed that he had a further serious rival in his friend Fritz Wahle, a painter who was engaged to Martha's cousin Elise but was also a brotherly friend to Martha herself, taking her out and helping and supporting her in a variety of ways.[103] He is said to have animated discussions with Martha about art history and recommended her certain books on the subject. Martha, who found their relationship interesting and enjoyable, had at least once allowed her near-cousin to kiss her – and this was after she had met Sigmund Freud. When he heard this, Freud was greatly alarmed.

Martha's friendship with Wahle had long since become a nuisance to him, but liberties of this order were a different matter entirely. Wahle had clearly assumed that his relationship with Martha would not essentially change on account of her engagement, and Martha had apparently done nothing to disabuse him in this assumption: everything was to stay just as it had been before. Freud learnt from Ignaz Schönberg that Wahle had adopted an improper tone in his behaviour towards Martha, and had been going about complaining that she was neglecting him and her letters were lacking in warmth. An affront indeed. Schönberg invited his two rivalrous friends to talk things out in a coffee house, but this only made matters worse. Wahle behaved oddly, seemed disgruntled, and threatened to kill first Freud and then himself if Freud did not make Martha happy. Freud failed to recognize the seriousness of the situation and laughed out loud, prompting a defiant Wahle to claim that Martha would immediately leave Freud if he so requested. Freud took little notice of this claim either. Wahle refused to yield and called for pen and paper to write her a letter there and then. When Freud insisted on reading it, the blood rushed to his head. The letter was addressed to 'Beloved Martha' and spoke of 'undying love'. So everything was to stay as it was, was it! Freud tore the letter to pieces, and Wahle stormed off, deeply upset. His friends followed him and tried to bring him to his senses, but Wahle was sobbing inconsolably. This in turn moved Freud to tears, and he took his friend by the arm and escorted him home. Yet the penny had dropped: Fritz Wahle loved Martha too. Sigmund confronted his fiancée with what had gone on, but Martha again protested that Wahle was only a friend, and refused to countenance any other interpretation. Even so, Freud could not get the thought out of his mind that Wahle might be right and that he, Freud, would lose her. The very idea drove him to a state of distraction in which he spent hours on end wandering through the streets at night.[104]

The conflict smouldered on for weeks after these melodramatic scenes, and the relationship between the young couple was extremely tense. Further discussions followed. Martha was evasive and unforthcoming. She had no intention of giving up her friendship with Wahle, but Freud's inordinate jealousy and wounded

Martha Bernays, about 1880

vanity in the end forced her to. Ever his mother's golden boy, Freud acted 'like a beloved only child whose position is being undermined by the arrival of a sibling'.[105] Martha might have been his princess, but he had his doubts whether he was her prince.

The question is whether Martha really saw herself as a fairy princess. For all the passion of her admirers, she was not very sure of herself. Despite certain statements to the contrary, she apparently had serious doubts about how attractive she was and complained – perhaps with a certain coquetry – of how little effect she had on men. It remains uncertain whether the struggle between the two enamoured friends held any appeal for her. She seems at least not to have been unreceptive to compliments. Yet her future husband did little to boost her ego or indulge her romantic illusions. Although he let his sensitive young bride know how much he liked her, it was not long after the engagement before he was bluntly holding forth about the transience of beauty and the importance of inner values: once the smoothness and bloom of youth had gone, he wrote, beauty was to be found only where goodness and understanding 'transfigure the features', and 'that is where you excel'.[106] Well intentioned this may have been, but it must have stung an insecure twenty-one-year-old who wanted to please the man she loved and was engaged to. As though nature had wanted to preserve her 'from the danger of being merely beautiful', he wrote in another letter, Martha's nose and mouth were shaped 'more characteristically than beautifully, with an almost masculine expression, so unmaidenly in its decisiveness'.[107]

Her strikingly pale complexion and the deep shadows under her eyes often gave Freud cause to pass on useful tips: Martha should get out more into the fresh air, drink red wine, and take Blaud's iron pills,[108] as many anaemic-looking girls were being advised at the time. He worried whether Martha's jaded looks might have something to do with the ardour of his embraces on the rare occasions they met, which were always under such unsatisfactory circumstances.[109] In spite of his characteristic analytical skills, it apparently did not occur to him – or only late on – that Martha's permanently sickly appearance might perhaps be a product of her state of mind or worries that were depriving her of sleep. Did she write to him of such matters? In one letter during their engagement Freud asks: 'why do you want to leave home? [. . .] Please unburden your heart to me once more. Could I possibly have become too inattentive to understand your subtly implied wishes [. . .]?'[110] Why indeed did she want to leave home? Was this something she had been vaguely yearning for, or were there other reasons? Perhaps Martha suffered more than Freud suspected from the tiring conflicts produced by the incompatible expectations and demands of her mother on the one hand and her fiancé on the other. Perhaps Freud's surmise – or fear – that she might 'have once more got used to Mama'[111] hinted at the distressing discord and antagonism in the triangle Martha formed with Sigmund and

Emmeline. Freud's comment implies that Martha had at some point previously grown 'unused' to her mother and that, having at that point felt confident of his influence over Martha, Freud now sensed that she was once again yielding to the sway of her mother, bowing to her authority in the usual manner. Martha was caught up in a furious tug-of-war between her fiancé and her family.

In addition, there were periodic tensions and feelings of estrangement in her relationship with Sigmund. In May 1886, at a critical time towards the end of their engagement, Martha wrote, 'You now always only write once about each thing, and then nothing more however much I ask, I'm not used to this from you my good man, it is certainly high time I brought you to heel, otherwise I'm quite sure to go completely thin and green for sheer annoyance and expectation.' It can only be conjectured what was really going on inside Martha, and how much she was suffering on account of a situation that was anything but unproblematic. By the same token, one can only speculate why Freud kept on urging his fiancée to eat more nourishing food,[112] whether she really did eat too little at times and even showed anorexic tendencies or whether 'Freud was simply trying to make her conform to his ideal of voluptuous femininity'.[113] Did Freud basically want less a beautiful wife – one who knew what she was worth and consciously aroused the erotic desire of other men – than one who was fixated on him alone? If so, then it was in his interests to put Martha in her place in certain respects. This he did when he went into raptures about Mademoiselle Charcot, the young daughter of his much-admired teacher, in one of the letters he wrote during his time in Paris. It did not fail to have its effect on the less than self-confident Martha, whose jealousy was duly appeased by Freud's subsequent protestations of love.

Though at the beginning of the relationship Martha 'must have been a self-assured and independent young woman',[114] episodes of this sort – together with Freud's sharp reproaches and the clear rules of conduct he sometimes wrapped up in a jocular tone – all had the effect of undermining her sense of self-sufficiency and spirit of opposition. In 1884, she once commented on the complete lack of independence in the behaviour and thought of a twenty-six-year-old cousin of hers. At that point *she* was different and made no secret of the fact that she had no intention of letting Sigmund influence her. Freud accordingly found her 'hard and reserved' and felt he had 'no power' over her because she was 'so fully matured' and 'every corner' in her was 'occupied'.[115] This had on the one hand appealed to Freud, who told her, 'this resistance of yours only made you the more precious to me',[116] but on the other it also made him 'very unhappy', and he was keen to keep her defensive attitude in check. Shortly after their engagement he was sneering at her attempts to put her foot down and hoping she would lose every trace of her 'tartness'.[117]

The issue of Martha's lack of self-esteem raises a number of questions. Was her low self-respect a reflection of the derogatory attitude of the time towards women? As the sort of woman who suppressed a lot of her feelings, how did she view her mother's tendency to vent not only her grief and sorrow but also more aggressive emotions? How did she cope with disappointment, anger and aggression herself? There is no indication that she ever gave expression to such feelings. She is more likely to have drawn attention to her state of mind by passive aggression or refusals to cooperate. She is said never to have lost countenance, strange though this might have seemed in certain situations. So did she turn her aggression against herself? Did she suppress it? Perhaps her moral severity and discipline were a form of self-imposed punishment. Such considerations also shed a different light on her relationship to her sister Minna, which was always described as harmonious: 'there was never a cross word between us', as Martha put it. After all, Minna did rather oust her from her place at her husband's side.

What is beyond dispute is that Martha conformed to the stereotype of a woman in a patriarchal marriage. Her husband held the view that for a woman a successful life inhered, broadly speaking, in submission to the man's goals and objectives, and he was on the whole in good company in thinking this. Martha herself did not consider it her destiny to have a career of her own. But was she really at such a disadvantage in her relationship with Freud, highly demanding as he is known to have been?

The insistence with which she clung on to Sigmund Freud, who was not exactly welcome to her family, perhaps provides a clue.

Many young women of the time in comparable circumstances would have bowed to their parents' will or simply been forced to back down. In spite of her social background and orthodox upbringing, Martha proved to be relatively independent, assertive and unconventional. As her daughter Anna Freud put it, 'my mother observed no rules, she made her own rules.'[118] One example of her lifelong wilfulness was the quirk she retained even in London of systematically ignoring the red lights at pedestrian crossings: as an elderly lady, Martha would simply make a beeline for the other side of the road and take it for granted that the drivers knew it was ladies first.[119] Her tenacity did not make her loud-mouthed, and on occasion she preferred to adopt an indirect approach. Nevertheless, the 'diplomatic skill' that she was often said to display concealed a genuine aversion to conflicts. She avoided open arguments and only made a stand when there was no alternative. She then often achieved more than she was able to when she took a more moderate line.

It was this mechanism that made her marriage possible and underlay the harmony that was to inform it. Martha was generous in marking out the bounds of what she found acceptable but all the more stubborn in her defence of these bounds. The fact that even as a young girl she had been confronted with unconventional ideas, changing circumstances, adversity and ill fortune stood her in good stead. The resulting emotional stamina and stress-resistance not only prepared her to be a patient fiancée and a disciplined and self-sacrificing mother of six, but also equipped her to deal with the tests and twists that life with her husband had in store for her, to stand up to controversy and hostility, and cope with the avalanches of protest sparked by his spectacular discoveries. This cannot always have been easy. Alongside the relatively harmless-sounding dismissals of psychoanalysis as unscientific, an 'art of interpretation' or 'play with words and concepts',[120] the congresses of the time were often unanimous in their condemnations of psychoanalysis as wretched 'old wives' psychiatry', a 'psychological epidemic among doctors who belong in a madhouse', a matter for the police to take care of, or simply a 'load of utter filth'.[121]

Cupid's Arrow

Freud met Martha Bernays at a time when her family circumstances were straitened by the death of the father. Martha's brother
and various relatives had assumed financial responsibility for the
family, but even so – like the Freuds – they were forced to tighten
their belts. They lived in modest conditions, and the pennies had
to be counted. The most important thing was to find a good match
for the girls. The parents had scrimped and saved to bring them
up and provide them with a decent education, and now the time
had come for the seeds to bear fruit. As Minna, four years younger
than Martha, was not yet of an age for such considerations to
apply, the family pinned all their hopes on the elder daughter.
Martha had been groomed to spend her life alongside a man of
means, and to her mother's satisfaction there was no shortage of
promising candidates. Emmeline Bernays was determined not to
throw away the card she had carefully kept up her sleeve. Yet her
daughter did not play along quite as she might have hoped.

Martha met her future husband in April 1882, when she was
almost twenty-one and Freud was going on for twenty-six. She
had been invited to stay at the Freuds' house by his sisters.
Martha's mother – with her two daughters fast growing into
young women – had probably been a welcome visitor to the Freud
household for some time previously. Sigmund had not yet
been introduced to Fräulein Martha, but it could only be a matter
of time.

Unlike other evenings, the young doctor on this occasion did not
immediately disappear into the 'cabinet' where he had his meals
and to which he usually withdrew to attend to his studies and
intellectual interests. It was the presence of the young lady visitor
that held him back. The 'first sight of a little girl sitting at a well-
known long table talking so cleverly while peeling an apple with
her delicate fingers' had 'disconcerted [him] lastingly'.[122] He was
seized by a strange feeling of confusion and could hardly take his
eyes from her. All resistance was in vain: it was love at first sight.
Martha too was deeply impressed. Freud devoted himself single-
mindedly to winning the unusual German girl's heart. He knew
what he wanted. Their fates were sealed.

Though rather awkward and shy to begin with, Freud was sure of his feelings for her and soon embarked on his courtship. Every day he sent her a red rose accompanied by a poem in Latin or some other language, and he compared her effusively to a fairy princess from whose lips fell roses and pearls.[123] Yet this was as far as he allowed himself to get carried away, and on the whole he did not exactly shower her with romantic compliments.[124] He preferred to invite her for walks, the two of them cosily strolling down from the Kahlenberg arm in arm. It was the end of May 1882 before they were able to exchange a few words in private. These words raised Sigmund's hopes, yet the very same day Martha refused to accept a bunch of oak leaves he tried to give her. He was very disappointed, and henceforth had an aversion to oak trees.[125] Yet this by no means put an end to his starry-eyed fantasies. The next day they went for a stroll with Martha's mother Emmeline in the Viennese Prater, where Freud showed himself keen to know more about her. Back home, Martha recounted the episode to her sister, insistently asking her what she made of it. In view of the position Minna was later to assume within the Freud household, her reply was almost prophetic: 'It is very kind of *Herr Doktor* to take so much interest in *us*.'[126]

On 8 June Freud's confidence was briefly dampened when he found Martha busy making a wallet for her cousin Max, and for a while he believed all his hopes to be dashed. But it was a false alarm: before long she was once again as charming as ever. Her kindness, warmth and attentiveness completely won him over. He was enchanted by the small, unexpected gestures with which she showed him how highly she regarded him, whether it was a cake she had baked him (custom obliged them to give each other a present after they had come across what the Viennese call a *Vielliebchen*, a double-flowering almond, on one of their strolls together) or a flowering twig.[127] Freud enjoyed being spoilt in this way, especially since he otherwise always had to be conscientiously thinking of the well-being of his own family. This girl, it seemed, would do him good, and it was not long before he was picturing a future spent together with her.

Martha's feelings were similar. The young man had made a great impression on her from the outset, particularly since – as Freud liked to be told – he reminded her of her father.[128] Delicately but

The Freud family, about 1878
From left to right, from back to front:
Pauli, Anna, Sigmund, Emanuel (Freud's half-brother), Rosa, Mitzi, Simon Nathansohn
(Amalie Freud's cousin), Dolfi, unidentified, Amalie Freud, Jacob Freud, Alexander, unidentified

unequivocally, she gave him to understand that his feelings were requited. Writing him a note to thank him for his *Vielliebchen* gift of *David Copperfield*, she signed it familiarly for the first time using her first name alone. When Martha was invited to dinner at the Freuds' house two days later on 13 June 1882, Sigmund took her name card as a souvenir, whereupon she squeezed his hand under the table, a gesture that did not go unnoticed by Sigmund's sisters, who drew their own conclusions. Shortly afterwards, Martha announced she had a little present for him. Freud was beside himself with joy, and the very same week plucked up courage to declare his love to her. Things were getting serious. He wrote his first letter to her: 'Dear Martha, how you have changed my life.'[129] She accepted and as a token of her affection gave Sigmund a ring that had belonged to her father, a smaller copy of which Freud then had made for her. Their engagement was settled.

Four weeks later, this very ring then suffered a mishap that distressed Freud considerably. He came to Martha asking the 'tragically serious question' of whether by any chance she had been 'less fond' of him that day, or whether she had been 'annoyed' with him or even 'untrue' to him. The soldered joint of the ring was broken, and the pearl mounted in it had fallen out. More or less the same thing happened the following year, and this time the pearl was lost. The year after that Martha gave him a new ring, also with a pearl. She got her engagement ring, a plain one bearing a garnet, in December 1883, once Freud had managed to raise the necessary money.[130]

By 17 June 1882, just two months after meeting for the first time, they considered themselves engaged. Yet it remained a secret, for they intuited that a formal betrothal would not have been a wise move at the time. Freud never officially asked for Martha's hand in marriage. After all, there was no intransigent father from whom the daughter had to be wrested (which might well have reinforced Freud's sensation of being her 'only' intended). Yet the main reason was another: the decisive obstacle was Martha's dominant mother, who seriously doubted whether Freud was the right man for her daughter. For the time being, therefore, there was no more than a furtive vow between Sigmund and Martha, though this did nothing to stem the flood of their emotions.

Of course, it was difficult to keep the engagement secret among their closest friends. They took a few particularly discreet ones into their confidence, and these promised not to breathe a word of the affair. Precautions had to be taken to make sure it stayed a secret. Martha's old friend Fritz Wahle, whose letters would not arouse any suspicion since he was himself engaged to be married, thus addressed a supply of envelopes to Freud for Martha to use, with only an unobtrusive 'M' in the top right-hand corner on the back betraying who the real sender was. Moreover, Martha's letters to Freud were not to be sent to his home. They decided that a better idea was for them to reach him through the laboratory assistant in Ernst Brücke's physiology institute, where Freud worked.[131] They could not be too careful. One meeting with a group of friends in a coffee house had a fretful Freud on the edge of his seat lest the five friends who knew of the liaison – including Fritz Wahle and Ignaz Schönberg – spill the beans to the four who did not. When his sister Rosa asked him whether he wrote to Martha, he denied doing so. A few days later the sisters got wind of the engagement anyway and were thus in on the secret whether Sigmund and Martha liked it or not.[132]

For all this initial secretiveness, Freud's successful courtship was an exceptional triumph, a double victory over at least two obstacles. First, he had landed – as he called her – a 'princess', for Martha came from a family with a higher social standing than his, a family with prestige but no wealth. Freud had neither.[133] Further, even though she was from a strictly religious family she had decided to share her life with a self-confessed atheist. For Freud such commitment must have seemed among other things a triumph over religion, which he regarded as a form of superstition, and a sign not only of her love but perhaps also of her willingness to make sacrifices.

A key factor was also that Martha was not from Vienna. Her origins in 'distant' Hamburg represented the universe that stretched beyond the confines of Vienna, a universe that Freud created in his dreams and that he needed for his research.[134] She symbolized what was yet to come, and what he intended to conquer. Yet there was still a long way to go. It was too soon to feel fully satisfied or at ease, for though he had been surprisingly

Martha Bernays during her engagement, 1884

quick in winning over his 'darling' he was far from having secured the blessing of her good mother, and this did not bode well. He was painfully aware that he was not regarded highly as a suitor, and took it for granted that his scheming future mother-in-law would do all she could to prevent an official betrothal.

Future events were to prove him right. Her first trick was to separate him from his beloved, or so it seemed to him. First of all Martha spent a long holiday in Wandsbek at the house of her uncle, by profession a broker in government bonds and a member of the governing body of the Jewish community. When Martha returned to Vienna in September 1882 her brother came to pick her up from Hamburg – with Freud living in fear that the secret visit he had paid Martha shortly beforehand would be found out. Indeed, if Eli had chanced to stay at the same Wandsbek hotel as Freud had during his flying visit and had happened upon Freud's name in the hotel register, he would have only needed to add two and two together. Yet fortunately Eli, who could afford a better hotel, had preferred to put up at one in Hamburg.[135] Freud's visit on this occasion went undiscovered, and for once at least being short of money worked to his advantage.

The second trick to thwart their liaison was not long in coming: Mama Emmeline made up her mind that the family was to return once and for all to Hamburg or Wandsbek. She had always missed her native city and never felt completely at home in Vienna, but in all probability it was other considerations that proved decisive. Freud suspected that there was a scheme involved. He was convinced that Emmeline had taken it into her head to foil her daughter's undesirable relationship with an impecunious and, what was more, atheistic young doctor, who in her eyes was anything but a good catch. Freud's biographer Ernest Jones,[136] by contrast, regarded tensions in the relationship between mother and son as a more important reason for the move. What is beyond question, however, is that Emmeline Bernays had other notions of what befitted Martha's station than this bond with a poor devil who possessed little more than good intentions, half-baked plans and a head full of romantic notions. For her it was not enough that the ambitious, cultured and outwardly self-confident young man had every chance of pursuing an outstanding career. No, her daughter's impoverished suitor first had to prove that he was capable of feeding a family. There was no mistaking that – to put it mildly – he was not received with open arms, and this was hurtful to Freud. Yet he resolved not to give in to his future mother-in-law and her machinations without a fight. His characteristic amalgam of independence of spirit, self-esteem, courage and controlled rage[137] here stood him in good stead. Being condemned to opposition was something he had been familiar with ever since his confrontations with anti-Semitic fellow students, if not before. Freud had never been afraid to put up a struggle, and he was not afraid to do so now.

In a long-drawn-out trial of strength, he did everything possible to wrest Martha from what he saw as the detrimental influence of her domineering mother and her equally obstructive brother, and to tie her to him once and for all. Yet the first round of the contest went to the wilful mother-in-law, who successfully pushed through her intended return to Hamburg. At first, neither Martha nor Sigmund had actually taken her plan too seriously. This was a mistake. Eli did not return to his home city, possibly because in Germany he would have been liable for military service.[138] Indeed, he was down on the 'defaulter' list for the 1860 age group, which meant he had undergone his medical and been found fit for service.[139] However, the two underage daughters – both of them (secretly) engaged – had no alternative but to follow the mother. Even though Emmeline's authoritarian decision ran counter to her own interests, Martha viewed it not as selfishness but as an attitude to be respected and accepted.[140] There was no choice: the young couples were provisionally to part company. Sigmund reproached Martha for not resisting her mother's plans vigorously enough.[141] Martha herself later[142] explained that her mother had virtually abducted her to Hamburg and demanded that she stay there until the marriage, arguing that with long engagements it was better for the couple to live apart. Martha made no secret of the admiration she felt for her mother's firm action.[143] The only thing that might possibly have impressed her more would have been if Sigmund had somehow succeeded in frustrating these plans. Yet he saw no other option than to let her depart, for which she in turn reprehended him. Freud responded in a letter: 'You must not say that I shouldn't have let you go.'[144]

Before Martha finally moved to Wandsbek, she used to visit Freud in his lodgings in Vienna's General Hospital, where he was working. Her first visit was a solemn moment, because – following his quarrels with Eli – Sigmund had for some time refused to visit his fiancée at her family home, and for weeks the only place they had been able to meet was the Freuds' cramped flat, where they could hardly be alone together, or the streets.[145] To keep Martha informed of the details of his day-to-day existence, he not only described his lodgings to her in words but also drew her a diagram of them. Much more than a mere outline of the room, this sketch included the positions of his bed, wardrobe and desk, but also, more curiously, certain terms that Freud applied to the walls. One of the long sides was called the 'animalistic side', while opposite it was the 'vegetative side' of the room. It is not too difficult to surmise what he meant. By 'vegetative' he understood all activities oriented towards the maintenance of the body: resting, sleeping and eating. The 'animalistic' aspect of his furnishings embraced everything that went beyond the merely existential: reading, studying and edification; in other words bookshelves, desk and pictures. This microcosm was rounded off with what he called the 'air and light side', comprising the window, as well as the 'outside world side', with the wardrobe and a double door. Before Martha 'graced' the room with her presence,[146] Freud wanted to make it more homely and asked her to embroider him two 'votive tablets' to hang above his desk. He opted for the inscriptions *Travailler sans raisonner* (Work without reasoning) and *En cas de doute abstiens-toi* (When in doubt abstain), both of which he held dear. When he opened his private practice three years later, he again asked Martha for an embroidery, this time a saying used by Charcot: *Il faut avoir la foi* (One must have faith). This was an adage that was always close to his heart.

Wandsbek

So it was that in 1883 the Bernays, mother and daughters, returned to Wandsbek[147] near Hamburg, moving into Hamburger Strasse no. 38.[148] Together with other properties in the area, the then small village of Wandsbek had been acquired in 1762 by the wealthy merchant Baron Heinrich Carl von Schimmelmann, quickly developing into a flourishing factory town, which soon even had its own castle.[149] At Schimmelmann's request, part of the large castle grounds was made open to the public: a tract of woodland where a century later Martha and her fiancé were to take such pleasure in their frequent strolls. In 1861 the castle fell victim to the plans of a property speculator, and the grounds were divided up again. A depot was built for the track-based 'horse railway', which from 1866 onwards was to provide travellers with a convenient connection between Hamburg city centre and Wandsbek. On his visits to Martha, Freud is likely to have used this modern and popular suburban service to reach his fiancée as quickly as possible. Wandsbek's waste lands also provided a site for one very special attraction that from 1881 was to draw hordes of visitors: the first artificial ice-rink in Germany.[150] During her years in Wandsbek, Martha too dreamed of gliding over the mirror-like surface, a diversion at the time regarded as highly un-ladylike, indeed thoroughly improper. If the lady was unlucky enough to lose her footing, even several layers of clothing might not be enough to stop bare leg being exposed to the general view. Accordingly, Freud was quick to let his fiancée know that vigor-ous winter activities of this sort were not for her, and categorically forbade her to go ice-skating, not out of fear she might sprain an ankle or break a bone but because he could not bear the thought of her being arm in arm with another man.[151] Three days later, he gave way and allowed her to go skating, but only under the con-dition she should skate unaccompanied.[152] Times were soon to change. When it came to his daughter Mathilde, Sigmund clearly no longer had any qualms about the pastime. Martin Freud described how he would go skating with Mathilde on a frozen pond in Vienna's Augarten Park, his pretty sister gathering no end of young gallants around her as she went along.[153]

Martha spent her years of engagement in Wandsbek in keeping with convention. She helped her mother, who also had a char-woman, in the running of the household, visited her circle of relatives and friends, and pursued her cultural interests. Above all, she spent a good deal of her time reading. Accompanied by her mother and sister, she would occasionally go to see a play or concert in nearby Hamburg. Such activities were punctuated by moments of pining for her faraway fiancé, especially whenever one of his letters arrived. She kept herself tirelessly busy with needle-work and worked on her trousseau, little suspecting that many of

Wandsbek, Hamburger Strasse, 1913

Martha lived here with her mother and sister during her engagement

the ornate crocheted covers would later serve them well during the First World War, when they were bartered for cigars and other goods in short supply.[154]

In the summer of 1883 Martha had a holiday break in Düsternbrook near Kiel, where she stayed at a guest house run by a gardener,[155] the object of Freud's envy for being at such close quarters to her. Freud was utterly sceptical whenever his 'wandering princess' undertook a short journey with her sister on her own initiative. 'Fancy, Lübeck! Should that be allowed? Two single girls travelling alone in North Germany! This is a revolt against the male prerogative!' was his rather sour comment on the enterprise shown by the two girls on another occasion. It was the beginning of the realization that being without a man did not mean being lonely, he went on, adding with a wry touch of *Schadenfreude*, 'Haven't you had any adventures? I would rather have enjoyed that.' Finally his tone became more conciliatory, and he admitted he had no choice but to express his pleasure 'that you got along so well in Lübeck, which I do herewith'.[156]

The following years of separation, during which they were able to see one another only rarely, were extremely painful for both of them. It felt as though they were oceans apart. Money was scarce. They were unable to inform each other directly and without delay of their worries and cares, and now that Martha was away Freud – who both personally and professionally was constantly venturing into troubled waters – was deprived of his only comfort. Freud needed her for his own balance. Time and again she had given him fresh heart in moments of despondency, showing him that he had her unstinting support. At the same time, however, she also represented an outlet for his aggressions and his dissatisfaction with himself and the world: to her he could bare this side of his character without it unduly upsetting her. There was also the further question of coping with the grudge he bore the mother-in-law (in all but name) who had put him in this situation in the first place.[157] Martha's plight was that of a bride-to-be who had to wait and trust to the future. She often felt lonely in spite of the company of her mother and sister at home and her lively social contacts.

When Sigmund visited his fiancée, he generally stayed for several days or weeks at a time and usually put up at the Wandsbek

Post Hotel.[158] At the beginning of their relationship, when Freud was anything but well liked by Martha's family, their main job was to find ways and means of meeting without any of her vigilant relatives getting on to them. Now and then one of Martha's friends would act as go-between, yet it was always difficult to arrange their secret rendezvous, and on one occasion it took days for Martha to set up a meeting on the sly.[159] Playing hide-and-seek like this was a demoralizing experience, and there were moments of dejection and despair. Freud once asked Martha whether it might not be better to take a year's 'probation', in other words consider their engagement as provisional for such a period, but Martha dismissed this faint-hearted proposal as 'nonsense'.[160] It later emerged that Freud's suggestion had been meant to put Martha to the test. Had she accepted his pragmatic proposal they would have certainly split up for good after a week.

In his efforts to wean Martha away from the influence of her mother and take her under his own wing instead, Freud even considered what was at the time a rather unusual step: his idea was to bring Martha to Vienna even before their marriage, asking his friend Ernst von Fleischl-Marxow if he could find a suitable job for her.[161] Martha gave the idea serious thought: indeed, she felt, it was no bad idea at all. Yet in her positive reply to Freud's suggestion she made a couple of blatant gaffes. First, she suggested she might live with her brother while she was looking for a job in Vienna – at a time when Sigmund was at loggerheads with Eli! Secondly, she applauded Freud's plan because it would ease the financial burden on her mother – as though that was what really mattered! What counted was the two of them: what did he care about Emmeline's finances! In that case, he sneered, Martha might as well take on any old job, even one in Hungary.[162]

Later, once the mood had grown more conciliatory, the couple also made formal appearances, for example at the theatre in Hamburg.[163] Martha cooked for him, but at her mother's behest was not allowed to take his meals to him in the hotel, which was done by the Bernays's cleaning lady. In this way, Martha not only commended herself as a future wife, but also helped limit the expenses of her notoriously penurious sweetheart during his stay. The relentlessly stern mother-in-law gradually seemed to be yielding. Perhaps she was impressed by Freud's tenacity. Martha too continued to show 'tact, forbearance and sheer emotional staying power',[164] as well as an unwavering disposition: she never doubted his deep love for her and was convinced of their future happiness. Only rarely did she succumb to despondency, anxious that her sweetheart might leave her to marry some professor's daughter and secure his financial and professional future at one fell swoop. Then it was up to him to raise her spirits, warning her against capitulating in the face of her only rival, science.

Yet other obstacles posed a greater threat. Martha and Sigmund had constant money worries, and in moments of gloom Freud judged that they might yet have to wait another ten or fifteen years. This thought was so unbearable that he once suggested they should marry in poverty, making do with two rooms and living on dry bread.[165] Years before their wedding, he asked her whether they should not simply get married on 17 June 1887, exactly five years after the day of their engagement, regardless of the circumstances. Martha consented, making him almost as happy as she had the first time he proposed to her.[166]

For some time now there had been more at stake than just this. For Freud, his bride-to-be was 'a symbol and a reflection of the challenge of winning and also keeping an established place in the world, in spite of the fear that things might change and go wrong'.[167] Nothing ventured, nothing gained: this was the idea. Indeed, he was prepared to go even further to achieve his goal. After long years of study – having taken his doctorate in 1881 and eked out a more or less penniless existence in the laboratory of Professor Ernst Brücke, in Freud's eyes the living ideal of professional self-discipline[168] – the young assistant in 1882 found himself obliged to rethink his professional interests and spoke with his supervisor about his future progress. Unwilling to raise his hopes, Freud's esteemed mentor put it to him straight. His desire for a career in scientific research was incompatible with a life-plan which included Martha. Bearing Freud's unsatisfactory financial situation in mind, Brücke urged him to renounce his academic ambitions and take up clinical activity. Freud understood. If he wanted to marry Martha, he had to create the financial basis to do so, and a private medical practice promised to be more lucrative than scientific investigation.[169] In the end it was Martha who set the course for the foundation of Freud's practice and thus the beginnings of psychoanalysis.

With the disillusioning counsel of Professor Brücke a world fell apart for Freud. For an ardent researcher, becoming a clinician was a painful sacrifice that was only compensated by the prize that beckoned. In fact, however, Freud's reluctant decision was to prove a new start and a crucial experience on the way to his real vocation. After all, a university laboratory could never have produced a patient like the 'Rat Man'.[170]

The Cocaine Episode: an Opportunity Missed

On the advice of his revered mentor Brücke, Freud left the laboratory for a future with Martha. Just a few weeks after getting engaged, he took up a lowly post as an *Aspirant*, or clinical assistant, in Vienna's General Hospital, where he remained for a total of three years, gathering a range of medical expertise by moving from department to department. The work never altogether caught his imagination, and here too he was soon drawn to research. After half a year he moved from Hermann Nothnagel's department of internal medicine to Theodor Meynert's laboratory for brain anatomy. As a compromise between theory and practice, he was now playing with the idea of specializing in neuropathology.

In May 1883 Freud rose to the position of *Sekundararzt*, and the summer of the same year saw a development that almost resulted in another major change of course. Freud had discovered a method of decisively improving microscopic images of brain slices by staining them with a gold chloride solution. His impressive histological findings were published, but his euphoric hopes of finding fame and fortune through science after all (and soon being able to marry) were dashed in the spring of 1884 at the latest, when a discussion with Nothnagel brought him back down to earth with a thud. Nothnagel did not share Freud's utopian ideas and thought the best thing would be for him to move to the provinces, make a fortune there, and perhaps return to Vienna at a later date. It was much more difficult to prosper in the capital. Freud's breakthrough was put on ice once again – and so was the wedding.

Yet Freud was not to be discouraged and soon recovered his confidence. A new project played a decisive role in this. Shortly before his sobering discussion with his supervisor, the young doctor had turned his attention to a new substance: cocaine. In the spring of 1884 he reported to Martha that he was interested in the properties of the as yet little-known drug. What he had heard about it sounded promising, though he realized nothing might come of it either.[171] He had read that the alkaloid powder derived from coca leaves, though not in common use, had been successfully employed by a German army physician to combat his soldiers' exhaustion. Further investigations revealed that South American Indians had for generations used coca as a stimulant, chewing its leaves from an early age, a habit that produced moderate pleasure without causing any apparent damage to their health. It was said that coca could help in the treatment of neurasthenia, as well as countering melancholy and increasing the appetite. Overwhelmed, Sigmund Freud resolved to ascertain the truth of these reports. If everything they said about cocaine was right, it might fill a gap in the possibilities for drug-based treatment in the realm of neurology. Freud set about looking into what this 'magical drug' could actually achieve.

He ordered the substance through the post from Merck of Darmstadt and started a programme of experiments on himself. As yet, he little suspected how addictive the euphoriant could be and was genuinely enthusiastic about its medical possibilities. Taking just a small amount of a solution of cocaine he felt noticeably better almost at once – somehow more relaxed, dynamic and efficient. In the days and weeks that followed he tried the same dose of cocaine on several occasions. He noticed an increase in self-control and vitality and a greater capacity for work without feeling dazed or in any other way dull-headed. He experienced the cheering effect of the drug as a lasting euphoria that in no way differed from the normal euphoria of healthy people, and found it difficult to believe he was under the influence of an intoxicant.

Not long afterwards, Freud was recommending the drug as a stimulant and generously distributing it among his friends so that others too might enjoy these synthetic delights. On a number of occasions he even sent a small dose to Martha, adding precise instructions on how to administer it. Martha promptly acknowledged receipt of the drug, thanked him warmly, and told him that, although she did not require any, she would divide it up as instructed and take some of it.[172] Otherwise so restrained in what she said and did, from time to time Martha thus guilelessly enhanced her sense of well-being with an invigorating pinch of cocaine. It helped her, she said, in moments of emotional strain, yet there is no evidence that she was ever addicted to it.[173] Freud's friend Ernst von Fleischl-Marxow, by contrast, whose attention Freud had drawn to cocaine in an attempt to relieve the chronic pains he was suffering, did fall victim to the drug. Freud began to realize that the chemical wonder weapon was a double-edged sword and that the effects of an overdose were frightful, though he himself continued to take it as a tonic at least until the mid-1890s.[174] 'We can only speculate why Freud, who was addicted to nicotine, did not develop an addiction to cocaine', his family doctor Max Schur later wrote about Freud's drug use.[175]

In spite of the tragic effect the drug had upon Fleischl-Marxow, Freud had every reason to believe he had achieved something big. Once he had gathered enough material he wrote the paper 'On Coca', in which he vehemently advocated broad medical use of the substance. He assumed that even if only half of these astonishing possibilities could be put into practice his name would be made for good. Once again, however, things were to turn out differently. His cocaine research did indeed hold the key to fame and fortune (and marriage with Martha), yet Freud failed to see how even when the answer was staring him in the face, for he did not pursue the most valuable of all its effects, which was as a local anaesthetic.

Once again, Martha played a decisive part in Freud's failure to seize his chance. He concluded his manuscript 'On Coca' with a vague recommendation for further investigation before rushing it off to the printer, for he had been granted a surprise holiday and wanted to reach Martha as soon as possible. He had not seen her for months.[176] Even though he had an inkling of some of the possible further applications, his own experiments with cocaine had to be shelved for the time being – too long, as it turned out. Others were to reap the rewards for the pioneering discovery of cocaine's potential as a local anaesthetic in eye operations, the Viennese ophthalmologist Carl Koller successfully testing the drug in the anaesthesia of the sensitive cornea. In a sense, it was Freud's yearning to see Martha that stopped him making his mark in the field of local anaesthesia. Towards the end of his life, he admitted that 'forty-nine years of wedlock' had 'compensated him for missing out on fame in his youth'.[177]

It was only with hindsight that Freud was able to view the cocaine episode – one of the opportunities that had got away – with such nonchalance. At the time, in 1885, it was the here and now that mattered: Freud had narrowly missed out on the breakthrough he was hoping for. He was now pushing thirty and was still not married to the woman of his dreams. Even so, he had some impressive scientific work behind him and, with the support of Professors Brücke, Nothnagel and Meynert, was in July 1885 appointed to the post of *Privatdozent* for neuropathology. Yet this was still no basis for marriage. Freud was unsure how much longer Martha would wait for him, while Martha for her part wondered how much longer she would have to be patient. As she approached her mid-twenties, people would be starting to regard her as an old maid. Yet no matter how they looked at it, there was little chance of marriage that year either.

The acid test of their relationship almost proved to be its undoing. Early in June 1885 Freud had taken on a post as locum in a private psychiatric clinic in Oberdöbling, just outside Vienna. It was an institution for members of high society, and Freud had to wear a top hat and white gloves in order not to look out of place. He enjoyed his new post, and asked Martha whether she might consider living there with him if all their high-flown plans came to nothing. It would not by any means be a bad option, and at last they would be able to marry. After toying with the idea for a while, Martha accepted.

This might almost have been the way things turned out. While he was working in Oberdöbling, however, Freud received some good news: in mid-June he was awarded a much-coveted travel grant for talented young *Sekundarärzte*, a decision that had hung very much in the balance due to in-fighting within the university committee. His intention was to use the princely sum of 600 gulden together with the six months' leave of absence for a study visit to the Salpêtrière in Paris. Freud had not been at all convinced that he would get the scholarship. Though he had bent over backwards to prepare the ground and win over protectors, he had never held out any great hopes. Martha, by contrast, had never doubted his success, indeed was taking it for granted. So convinced was she, in fact, that she even poked gentle fun at his zealous efforts to woo influential supporters.[178] She was not mistaken. With the grant in his pocket he could go to Paris, return to Vienna with the aura of a great scholar, and finally marry Martha. He did not think twice about it. After a six-week stay in Wandsbek, during the course of which he finally overcame Frau Bernays's objections to him, in October he headed for Paris, firmly resolved to make his fortune. Little did he suspect the repercussions this trip would have upon his and Martha's life.

Paris

The young *Privatdozent* arrived in Paris in mid-October 1885. His heart still brimming with the weeks he had spent with Martha in Wandsbek and the sadness of their parting, he felt uncertain and anxious about what lay in store for him. No sooner had he settled in than he set about exploring the city, gathering first impressions of the streets and churches, the theatres, museums and shops, the parks and the people out promenading. His letters to Martha contain vivid and detailed descriptions of what he saw and the impact of these early days in Paris. He wandered through the streets, strolled along the banks of the Seine, and admired the busy boulevards, above all the tree-lined Champs-Elysées with its elegant crowds and its carriages racing past. The architectural treasures dating back centuries made a particular impression on him. He told Martha of his astonishment at the obelisk from Luxor in the Place de la Concorde, and wrote of immense buildings and bridges, the spacious Bois de Boulogne and the quiet Tuileries Gardens. He delighted in the view from Notre Dame and took special pleasure in the Louvre, where he lingered over the ancient statues, gravestones, inscriptions and relics, and wondered at the great busts of emperors, colossi of kings, bas-reliefs and sphinxes, 'a dreamlike world'.[179] In the midst of all this beauty, however, Freud felt profoundly alone. How different it would have been if Martha could have been with him! The splendour of Paris made him painfully aware of his own limitations, his poverty, timidity and loneliness. He found it helpful to write Martha long letters in which he could confide how he felt to her. His thoughts revolved around his fears for the future, while his nervous excitement about studying with Charcot was a further weight on his mind. He was anxious about how they would receive an impoverished foreigner like himself.

Eventually the time had come: armed with his letter of recommendation from Vienna, he passed through the gateway to the celebrated Salpêtrière Clinic near the Gare d'Austerlitz. Under the leadership of Jean Martin Charcot, who had been appointed director in 1862, the Salpêtrière had developed from a psychiatric detention centre to a full hospital with a worldwide reputation.[180] Right from the outset Freud was won over – indeed quite dazzled – by the great professor. It was not just Charcot's powerful physical presence that impressed him, but also the courtesy and civility with which Charcot received him. To his great surprise, the imposing neurologist gave him a warm welcome without the least trace of presumption or arrogance.

Charcot became his 'master'. In Paris Freud had some of the most lastingly important experiences of his professional life. Professor Charcot's lessons were quite out of the ordinary. Doing the rounds with his assistants, he would allow himself to be introduced to patients suffering the most diverse of neurological disorders, would exchange a few words with them, make some impromptu reflections on the pathology in question and a preliminary analysis of the symptoms, decide upon a diagnosis and recommend a treatment. But this was not all. On top of this, he developed original aetiologies of the illnesses involved, and not only allowed but expressly encouraged his students to ask questions and raise objections, something that astonished and awed Freud. Charcot had faith in his own judgement and trusted what he saw, but would openly admit it if he made a mistake. His motto, a bon mot that Freud never forgot and was to make his own, was: *La théorie, c'est bon, mais ça n'empêche pas d'exister.* Theory is all very well, but that does not prevent facts from existing. This was perhaps the most important lesson Freud learnt.

Charcot's brilliant lectures were the Salpêtrière's principal attraction. The great lecture hall would always be filled to the very last seat with doctors, students, even writers and other curious onlookers. Charcot would enter punctually, often accompanied by visitors of renown, and a performance worthy of the theatre would take its course. The highly personal style and considerable dramatic skill with which he underscored his lectures and reconstructed complex pathologies made for an overwhelming show. The audience hung on his every word as he lectured, astounded by his daring theories of hysteria as an ailment that afflicts men as well as women, and spellbound again and again by his spectacular demonstrations with patients. Charcot was not just a great doctor but a great performer, too.

Freud was mesmerized. His initial despondency vanished, and his spirits revived. He began to feel more at home in the metropolis on the Seine, acquired a taste for Paris and the proverbial French light-heartedness, and opened himself to the city's charms. Though always short of money, he accompanied a colleague to see Sarah Bernhardt at the theatre[181] and went with a cousin of Martha's, Jules (Julius) Bernays,[182] to see *Le Mariage de Figaro* at the Comédie-Française, followed by a beer in a *brasserie*.[183] All this he shared with Martha through his letters, not even shrinking from bluntly telling her what her cousin John – whom he also met in Paris – was itching to know, namely whether he was keeping 'a mistress' in Paris.[184]

The weeks flew past. On 20 December 1885 Freud travelled to Wandsbek to spend his first Christmas with Martha and her family.[185] In spite of his constant shortage of funds, he had not only brought a fine gift of jewellery for his fiancée but also – as his journey took him via Cologne – bought some authentic eau de Cologne for her mother, and had not forgotten Minna. He even had something for the cleaning lady. After all this spending he had just enough money to pay for the rail ticket to Hamburg, where Martha was impatiently waiting for him. Over the holidays he kept his promise to tell her every last detail about life in Paris. To be undisturbed for a while, the two of them went on long strolls together in the Wandsbek woodland, where they talked and talked among the bare winter trees. Martha sensed the lasting impression that Charcot had made upon her sweetheart and could tell that Freud's career was about to take a new turn. The question was whether this would bring their wedding nearer and put an end to their trial of patience. There was nothing Martha yearned for more. Freud initiated his wife-to-be into his new plans. His idea was to look more closely at cases of hysteria while he was in Paris. Afterwards, he wanted to go to Berlin to study possible treatments for hysterical paralysis and investigate neurological diseases in children. His intention was then to return to Vienna in the spring and open a practice. As soon as he had gained a foothold and could assess his income, he told Martha, their thoughts could turn to marriage. Martha agreed. She assured him that she firmly believed in him and would support him to the best of her ability.

First, however, it was time for Martha and Sigmund to part again. Even so, Freud's remaining time in Paris did not seem so long now, and the start to the new year was a pleasant one. Charcot had entered into an agreement with Freud whereby the promising young doctor, who had long since attracted his attention, was given the task of translating his lectures into German. Freud was now one of the circle of favourites who were invited to receptions at the illustrious professor's magnificent residence. Charcot was not only at home in the world of medicine but was also regarded as a 'social lion',[186] and it was a great honour for Freud to be asked to one of the sumptuous soirées at his master's 'palatial' house.[187] He was of course introduced to Madame Charcot as well as to the pretty daughter of the house, who – to Martha's disquiet – did not fail to make an impression upon him. This time Martha was not impervious to a touch of jealousy. Freud duly prepared for what for him was an exciting and unusually chic occasion: after all, he was loath to make a fool of himself in such circumstances. In Hamburg Martha shared his anxiety that everything should go well. He paid meticulous attention to his outward appearance: his perfectly groomed hair, impeccable shirt, suitable tie and white gloves all matched his black tailcoat.[188] By his own account, he felt outwardly 'very fine', yet at the same time awkward and nervous. He tried to overcome his lack of self-assurance in tried and tested fashion – with a pinch of cocaine 'to untie my tongue'[189] – and set off for Charcot's house with his heart pounding. The evening promised entertainment and lively conversation, for in his 'magic castle', as Freud called it,[190] Charcot generally gathered together the most diverse of figures, including artists, men of letters, and eminent doctors. And a pleasant evening it was too. In one of his letters to Martha, Freud gave vent to his relief at not having made himself ridiculous in Charcot's presence. Further soirées followed, though not all equally stimulating, as Freud confided to Martha under the seal of secrecy: 'But please don't tell anyone how boring it was', he wrote, and sighed: 'Thank God it's over'.[191]

As his stay in Paris neared its end, Freud was pushing thirty, and the time was fast approaching for him to establish his livelihood and get married. Martha, his beloved Martha, had stood by him and waited for him all these years. In early March he confidently headed for Berlin, intending to spend a month there as a guest student. It was just a stopover: he did not demand a great deal of Berlin, he wrote from his lodgings in Karlstrasse, and 'then at last comes the decision'.[192]

At the beginning of April 1886 Freud returned to Vienna. His enthusiasm was mixed with a tangle of confusing emotions. He trusted in himself and believed in the future, but at the same time feared that his plan to marry Martha that very year might yet come to nothing. These doubts were not unfounded, for his prospects in the spring of 1886 were still as uncertain as ever. And yet the time was ripe to take the plunge and found his own practice. With a grim sense of humour he discussed the financial outlook for such an enterprise with his friend and colleague Josef Breuer, half-playfully toying with the idea that he might even emigrate and eke out his earnings as a waiter.[193] Freud decided against gastronomy and did the job properly. He resigned from his post in the General Hospital, moved for the first time into a flat of his own, and on Easter Sunday, 25 April, opened his surgery at Rathhausstrasse no. 7.

An elated Freud sent his first fee to Wandsbek, telling Martha to buy a plume for her hat and treat herself to a bottle of wine.[194] The money was in good hands with Martha, and now all she had to do was share his happiness.

Progress was being made. Breuer and Nothnagel sent him patients, though only some of these were paying customers.[195] He provided Martha with painstaking accounts of his income and outlay and frequently added descriptions of his patients. Even though quite a few of his treatments were given free of charge, within a short time of its opening the practice was doing well enough for them to be able to turn their thoughts to a date for the wedding.

And then came the bad news. Just when he had set up his practice and was starting to build up a core of regular patients, Freud was called up for several weeks of reserve duty military training exercises! It could hardly have come at a more inconvenient time: his patients would stop coming if he went a long time without holding a surgery. Despondent and downcast, Freud wrote to tell Martha of the unfortunate turn of events. She took the news unexpectedly pragmatically and calmly accepted what could not be avoided anyway. Her confident and imperturbable reaction gave Freud fresh heart. If she were dejected, she hardly let it show. The only thing she asked of him – without a hint of irony – was not to overexert himself in the scorching summer heat when he was marching.

Around the same time, Freud was trying to find a new place to live, and came upon an attractive offer: amply spacious, in a beautiful modern house, situated in a first-class location just off the Ringstrasse. But there was one snag. The magnificent house in which their flat was available had been built on the very site where hundreds of Viennese had met an agonizing death in the great fire that destroyed the Ring Theatre in December 1881. It had been the wish of Emperor Franz Josef to put the disaster behind them by raising a particularly striking new building on the site of the tragedy. Freud himself did not let these details unsettle him in the slightest and had no misgivings about moving into the elegant new house. He openly told Martha of the dilemma: the harrowing past history of the site on the one hand and the great opportunity it represented on the other. Martha had no reservations either. She immediately approved his intention to step in quickly and herself set about dealing with the patterns for the wallpapers and fabrics.

Emmeline Bernays was flabbergasted when she heard of the alarmingly advanced state of the wedding preparations. After all, she had been assuming that the wedding day would be considerably later, and certainly not before the winter. She did not understand how Freud could be thinking of such an early wedding when he had only shortly before been forced to interrupt his practice for several weeks and as a result faced a drastic loss of earnings. Outraged, she wrote her future son-in-law a letter charging him with irresponsibility and foolishness,[196] and upbraiding him for what in her eyes was the ill-considered and precipitate behaviour of a 'spoilt child'. It was not exactly a harmonious start to the kinship that was soon to be officially inaugurated, harking back to times they thought they had left well and truly behind them.

Yet Freud turned a deaf ear to the directions from his mother-in-law, and gradually the tide turned. His own meagre earnings and savings, the modest resources of his bride-to-be, wedding presents in cash from her family – from her aunt Lea Löwbeer in Brünn and her uncle Louis Bernays in London[197] – as well as loans and gifts from well-off friends, finally made it possible for Sigmund and Martha to marry. At the end of his month-long military exercise Freud returned to Vienna and immediately set off for Hamburg. The wedding was fixed for 13 September 1886.

Eli Bernays, Martha's Brother

All these changes – which were to prove decisive in the development of Freud's career – occurred within the four years of engagement documented by the famous *Brautbriefe*, the letters exchanged by the betrothed couple.[198] Even as an old lady Martha would look back on her years of engagement 'with a beatific smile that recalled her great happiness'.[199] Her sweetheart had been simply marvellous – quite perfect – in her eyes, and she had been his chosen one, the one he had fought to make his own. The two of them had been on an emotional roller-coaster taking them through the whole range of passions from the heights of happiness to the depths of despair, and it was a source of great pride to her later in life that they had not come unstuck in the course of their trials and tribulations. Freud proved to be someone who one minute was head over heels in love, romantic, intimate, impetuous and enthusiastic, and the next was depressed, didactic, restrictive, at times splenetic and more occasionally repentant and understanding. He was ruthless in his treatment of both his own and other people's feelings, and not even the tiniest of details escaped his notice. He revealed to Martha how he saw himself, what made him angry, where his doubts lay, what he wished for, what made him go sentimental or soft, what prompted him to dramatize matters or bully people, and what things he had to force himself to do.[200] He would heap reproaches upon her, criticize her, chastise her, and she would protest vehemently. He told her early on in their relationship that he did not want her to be a spineless toy doll, but was this just paying lip-service? 'Marty', he wrote, 'is no longer the eldest daughter, the superior sister: she has become quite young, a sweetheart only a week old'.[201] His maxim was that a woman should 'soften but not weaken a man'.[202] Freud saw a skirmish, among other things, as a constructive act that reinforced the ties between them: blood and troubles shared made the most enduring bonds, he claimed.[203]

From time to time Martha had the feeling that she failed to 'find the right words' or was colder than her future husband.[204] Indeed, when it came to ardour she could hardly compete with him. Freud believed that he loved her more and had loved her for longer than she loved him. To the end of their engagement he reproached her for having consented to marry him without returning the intense affection that he felt for her, alleging that he had gone through hell while she had been trying in vain to love him. There was no persuading him otherwise; it was virtually an *idée fixe*. In April 1884, he reproved her for the 'only wrong' she had committed: saying yes without being in love.[205] While Martha – in accordance with the dictates of propriety – was the more reticent of the two, Freud openly voiced his desires. This he did symbolically too, having sheets of writing paper specially printed with the intertwined initials of their first names on them. He wanted Martha all to himself, and everyone was to know it. From the very first day of their engagement, Freud treated anyone who felt responsible for Martha as an enemy: 'has it not been laid down since time immemorial that the woman shall leave father and mother and follow the man she has chosen? You must not take it too hard, Marty, you cannot fight against it; no matter how much they love you I will not leave you to anyone, and no one deserves you; no one else's love compares with mine.'[206]

He was only apparently joking when he referred to himself as a 'knight errant' on a pilgrimage to his 'princess' who was being kept locked away by her 'wicked uncle'.[207] Yet his unconditional desire to be with Martha was at odds with the reality of their separation. Crossed in their love, they decided to keep a joint diary, their own personal *Geheime Chronik* ('Secret Chronicle'), which they began in January 1883, when the two of them were still together in Vienna.[208] Freud and Martha took turns to write what was intended as a substitute for correspondence as well as a record for later days, a sort of cross between a diary and a personal confession. Their intention was to destroy their love letters and a diary kept by Freud on their wedding day, keeping the 'Secret Chronicle' alone as a document of this period of their life. But just over a year after starting it Freud complained that the chronicle had not been kept up, 'as a result of insufficient participation by one of us'.[209] And that was that.

At the time, Freud's love for Martha lived predominantly on paper and was nourished by memories, fantasies, hopes and dreams. Their unwanted separation – which first provided the scope for illusions – perhaps even contributed to the stability of their relationship in its early days. After all, it permitted and justified their vague pining for one another, while ensuring that they were not confronted with the consequences of actually fulfilling their dream of union. In his letters Freud thus passionately demanded to be near his faraway sweetheart, yet in the same breath had to forgo that very demand. This possibly helped him overcome his fear of human intimacy, a product of the unresolved bond that had tied the golden boy Sigmund to his mother.[210] This period brought to light how excessive Freud was by nature, and how little he had in common with the image of the serene scientist with which he is often associated.[211]

Freud's at times exaggerated demands that Martha should entirely renounce her family and friends for his sake met with healthy resistance on her part. One particular bone of contention that brought their relationship to within a whisker of breakdown just a few months before their wedding was the fact that Martha let her brother Eli manage and invest money that was hers, a state of affairs that aroused Freud's deep suspicion. Martha had entrusted her brother with part of her dowry from her uncle's legacy, and Freud believed that the cash that belonged to her would be locked away in a safe or placed in a bank account inaccessible to anyone else. Eli was a businessman, however, and had invested the money profitably with a view to earning interest and increasing its value. The only catch was that, lucrative though it was, the investment could not be converted into cash at short notice. Freud seemed to equate Eli's form of financial management with speculation, and the whole business struck him as dubious. Whether bank notes or bonds, in Freud's eyes money was money, and that was either there or – as was clearly the case now – it was not. When the news then reached him that Eli was in short-term financial difficulties, he feared the worst and told Martha to ask for her money back at once. Eli's answer was evasive. This came to Freud's ears and further compounded his mistrust, which shot out of all proportion. Insinuating that Eli had possibly even taken money from her uncle Jacob Bernays's legacy,[212] he came out with unpleasant comments about his future brother-in-law that Martha greatly resented, and told her to break off all relations with her brother immediately. An indignant Martha denounced this as an outrageous calumny, and assured Freud that Eli had never let her down in his life and they had no reason to doubt his integrity and honesty now: she was quite certain he had not embezzled their money and would pay back every last penny of it. Yet her remonstrations fell on deaf ears, for this confrontation with Eli – the old adversary whose aim was to thwart their union – had churned up long-dormant emotions inside Freud. What was more, Martha was not siding with her future husband in the matter, but had allied herself with the villain, leaving Freud in the lurch after all their years of exasperated waiting.[213] The last straw came when Eli then offered to step in and buy Martha and Sigmund the furnishings for their new home on his own account on hire purchase, and Martha did not even reject her brother's offer straightaway. The very idea of being dependent upon someone he did not trust an inch and who one day might impound his furniture and ruin his practice: it was madness!

Freud sent Martha an ultimatum, demanding that she should write her brother an angry letter in which she called him a scoundrel.[214] Martha was at her wit's end. Her fiancé was not joking: she was to make a choice one way or the other – yet she resisted the pressure. When Freud saw that this was not working either, he threatened to denounce Eli to his superiors at work, though he did come to think better of this idea. Instead, he took matters into his own hands and – without telling Martha – drafted an aggressive letter to Eli in which he made it perfectly clear how serious the situation was. This set the ball rolling. Somehow Eli got hold of the money and the next day sent it to his sister, though not without greatly lamenting her future husband's 'brutal' manners.

It was only now that Martha learnt of what Freud had done behind her back. She reproached him furiously for his unseemly behaviour and for making such a song and dance about 'a few shabby gulden'.[215] Perhaps she had her father's own financial misadventures in mind. For his part, Freud insisted that it was not the money so much as their hope of married happiness that had been at issue. She was not to write to him again until she promised to break off all contact with her brother. This, Martha admitted, was the first and only time she felt she no longer loved Freud. She was on the point of giving up all hope of a happy outcome. They were 'on the edge of an abyss'. Everything – the wedding, the whole relationship – was in danger, and it was solely thanks to Martha's 'tact and firmness' that they overcame the crisis.[216] The only thing that kept her going was the memory of how once before, years earlier, Freud had come back to her having left her in anger.[217] She trusted her conviction that his love would end up carrying the day over his aggressiveness.

Freud's bitter feud with Eli is all the more astonishing because in Vienna Martha's brother had been part of his circle of friends and acquaintances even before he and Martha were on close terms. For a while in July 1882 Eli even lived with the Freuds and was so friendly towards Sigmund in particular that Sigmund felt almost ashamed at not having confided to him that he had got

Eli Bernays
Martha's brother

engaged to his sister.[218] Eli was a charming character, it seems, and was regarded as open and generous. The two men were on good terms until the critical phase that began with the secret betrothal and degenerated into a campaign to crush the enemy entirely.

Eli started off with the advantage over Freud and was in a better financial position than anyone else from either of the two families. He edited a journal on economics and was an astute businessman. Following his father's death he considered it his duty to provide for his mother and two sisters, and subsequently he would also help out the Freud family. For a long time, however, Sigmund regarded him as a 'spoilt child',[219] perhaps because he took a more light-hearted approach to life than Sigmund did. But Eli was no woolly-headed dreamer. For what he took to be good reasons, Freud tried to drive a wedge between Martha and her family. He had fallen out with Eli in other matters as well. One of these had to do with the payment of Sigmund's brother Alexander (1866–1943), whom Eli had taken on as an apprentice.[220] Martha could not bear the thought of her headstrong sweetheart being on bad terms with her family and tried to calm him down, imploring him repeatedly to make concessions so it would not come to an irrevocable split. He did not find it easy, but for Martha's sake he made an effort and in October 1882 wrote Emmeline Bernays a letter in which, after paying her some formal compliments, he meticulously explained his point of view to her. It was hardly a masterpiece of diplomacy: Martha's mother tore it to pieces.[221] It was a long time before feelings cooled down again. It cannot be known for sure whether the eventual reconciliation was Martha's work, but she is likely to have played a major part in it.

Relations improved for a while following Eli's engagement to Sigmund's sister Anna. Eli Bernays was seen as a good match for Anna: he was not without means and enjoyed high social standing. Freud revised his opinion of Eli's complacency, appreciating that he must be a decent fellow to marry a penniless girl when he could have had any number of other women and done much better for himself.[222] Yet the peace did not last long. By March 1883 Freud's old hostility to Eli had come back to life, and matters were not made any easier by Eli's support for Emmeline's decision to return to Hamburg. For a long time the two old friends did not speak a word, a situation that Martha found unbearable. Their rift was so deep that Freud did not even go to Eli's wedding – with Freud's own sister – in October 1883. When Anna gave birth to their first child some eighteen months later, Freud waited for a moment when Eli was away before going round to congratulate her. The invective reached a climax with the financial dispute of 1886, and it was not until the 1890s that things began to change. In 1893 Eli and Anna Bernays emigrated to New York. Martha and her husband helped them financially through the early days and took one of the two daughters, Lucie, into their home until matters were more or less sorted out in the new country. A good year later, Lucie and her sister Judith, who had been staying with Sigmund's parents, in turn made the journey over to the United States.[223] From this time onwards, relations between the two men were much easier, which pleased Martha particularly, even though her brother now lived such a long way away. Family ties proved to be amicable across the Atlantic, and many years later it was the son of Eli and Anna, Edward Bernays, who translated and edited some of Freud's works for the US market.[224]

Till Death Us Do Part

According to Sigmund's sister Anna, Eli Bernays's wife, the four of them – Anna, Eli, Martha and Sigmund – had originally planned a romantic double wedding in Freud's parental home.[225] The plan fell through: Anna and Eli were already married by 1883. On 13 September 1886, the time finally came for Martha and Sigmund too.[226] The marriage certificate states that the witnesses were Gustav Malschafsky, 66 years old, of independent means, resident nearby at Hamburger Strasse no. 32, and Uncle Elias Philipp, aged 61. Martha later recalled the registrar's surprise at the ease with which she had signed her new name: perhaps, in her mind's eye, she had long since seen herself as Frau Freud. The religious ceremony was fixed for the following day, to be performed by Rabbi Dr David Hanover, head of Wandsbek Synagogue:[227] a civil wedding on its own was not officially recognized at the time in Austria. Atheist though he was, Sigmund gave in to the legal requirements that made the divine blessing necessary, and to his displeasure the bridal couple were wed under a *chuppa*, a wedding canopy that symbolizes not only the heavenly firmament but also the roof of matrimony. The Jewish wedding rite further involved the groom giving the bride a ring, as well as crushing a glass underfoot in recollection of the destruction of the Temple of Jerusalem.[228] The reluctant bridegroom had been initiated into all the ceremonial rules and prayers literally the night before by Uncle Elias. The ceremony was fixed for a weekday to ensure that only a few friends were available and the whole thing could proceed within a small circle of people. Instead of formal evening dress, it was enough for the groom to wear a frock coat and top hat.[229]

The wedding brought to an end a difficult engagement. Although Martha had repeatedly warded off Sigmund's frequent attacks on her values and personality, and had brought him to understand that victory over her would be tantamount to defeat for him, this did not apply to the question of faith. Indeed, religion was probably the most serious cause of tension between the two of them.[230] Martha insisted on her devotion, while Freud was not just an indifferent unbeliever but a principled and uncompromising atheist. In his own way every bit as doctrinaire as he accused her of being, Freud was set on winning his bride away from what he regarded as superstitious nonsense and mystic hocus-pocus. With an almost fanatical tenacity, he sought to make her abandon beliefs that she had never before even doubted and that had decisively shaped her childhood and youth. It angered him that she did not oppose her domineering, orthodox mother, and he tirelessly tried to goad her into doing so. Once when she was ill he thus advised her simply to eat 'in secret' – in contravention of the dietary laws that were strictly obeyed in the Bernays family.[231] Other religious customs that Martha liked to observe likewise met with his head-shaking disapproval: on the Sabbath, for example, when it was forbidden to write, she preferred to spare her mother's religious sensibility by writing her letters in fine pencil unobserved in the garden, rather than have the audacity to take up her pen in her mother's presence.[232]

It was situations such as these that prompted Freud to claim that they were in for a surprise at what a heathen he was going to make of pious Martha. In appearance at least, his prediction proved right, for on the whole Freud did impose his will. Within a short time of their wedding – at which Freud had bowed to tradition for legal reasons – he had ensured that the household they shared was not run on orthodox terms. The cooking was not kosher, and nor was Martha allowed to light the Sabbath lights: in other words, she had to renounce that important Jewish ritual that was traditionally carried out by the woman, the recital of the blessing.[233] It was only after the death of her husband over fifty years later that she lit the candles again for the first time.

Martha and Sigmund spent their honeymoon on the Baltic coast in Lübeck and Travemünde. In a joint letter written to Mama Emmeline on 15 September 1886, they jokingly referred to 'the first day of what we hope will prove a Thirty Years War between Sigmund and Martha',[234] and in general they enjoyed the togetherness and happiness for which they had waited so long. A new phase in their life had begun, in Freud's eyes posing a new threat to his place in her heart. The days of exclusive attention, he felt, were probably over: 'once one is married one no longer – in most cases – lives for each other as one used to. One lives rather with each other for some third thing, and for the husband dangerous rivals soon appear: household and nursery.'[235] He feared that, 'despite all love and unity, the help each person had found in the other ceases. The husband looks again for friends, frequents an inn, finds general outside interests.' Yet this 'need not be so', he added, as a hopeful coda to an otherwise rather cheerless disquisition on marriage.

After Brünn, where they visited their benefactress Aunt Lea, they travelled on to Vienna. Here, in October 1886, they moved into a flat in the so-called *Sühnhaus*, the 'house of atonement' that Emperor Franz Josef had had built at Maria-Theresien-Strasse no. 8. Freud's family gave Martha a warm welcome, and this made her new start in Vienna easier. The young woman did not make such heavy weather of getting on with her mother-in-law Amalie as Sigmund had done with his. As one of her nieces reported, the relationship between Martha and her mother-in-law had been perfect as far back as she could remember.[236]

The wedding was immediately followed by the next period of hard times. Money continued to be a problem. From the outset Sigmund had entrusted Martha with their budget, and it was she who had looked after their finances.[237] Indeed, he had made her his banker within a fortnight of their engagement, even providing

Wedding photograph, 14 September 1886

her with justifications for unnecessary expenditure such as choco-
late.[238] Martha knew how to keep house. A present she regarded
as too extravagant was unceremoniously sent back with the firm
words: 'You mustn't do that.'[239]

Money was a weight on their minds and had been for as long as they had known one another. It was for want of money that they saw so little of one another during their years of engagement, and it was for want of money that they had to delay their wedding. Frequently worried about the livelihood of his parents and sisters, Freud would sink into despondency whenever he was unable to give his Martha whatever gift he had in mind for her – jewellery, a hat or some fine garment. He himself likewise attached considerable importance to a good wardrobe: there were many things one could easily do without, but not a neat appearance, which in his eyes was a matter of self-respect. This requirement became a problem whenever finances were at a low ebb. The two of them together would weigh up whether he could afford a new suit or at least a tie. On one occasion Martha gave him one as a gift, so for the first time he had two good ties to call his own. Yet there continued to be periods when they lived from hand to mouth, and even after the wedding they had to keep on watching every penny. Although Martha had their finances under control and was careful and economical in keeping house, shortage of money would remain an issue for a long time to come. Freud had warned her of this, prophesying times of privation and no little sacrifice before the better future he confidently anticipated.

Freud's premonition turned out to be completely accurate. During October 1886 hardly a patient set foot in his practice. Earnings were nowhere near covering expenses, and making a joke of their plight did not solve it. Freud was obliged to pawn the gold watch his half-brother Emanuel had given him, and his wedding present for Martha, also a gold watch, would have met the same fate if Minna had not helped them out.[240] Yet gradually things began to look up. The practice picked up and began to flourish; the waiting room filled up; their worries became fewer. Life together was proving harmonious, and finally – by the beginning of 1887 – they were expecting their first child. Their dreams were starting to come true.

Vienna

Berggasse 19

In the *Sühnhaus* the young couple set up home together and created the domestic idyll that they had painted in such glowing colours during their engagement: two or three rooms, tables and chairs, beds, mirrors and a clock, an armchair, and linen tied up with pretty ribbons.[1] By the beginning of September 1891 three children had been born, and the family moved into the Berggasse. Martha was apparently not exactly bowled over by their new abode not far from the university quarter, but it was too late. Her husband had already signed the contract for the empty flat, which occupied an entire floor of house number 19.[2] Unfortunately, the flat was not very big, the staircase was rather steep, and the whole house was too dark. Martha was not particularly keen on the small, rather unprepossessing street in which it was located either, even though at the top end it bordered on an elegant district. The petit bourgeois neighbourhood was too down at heel for her taste: the lower part of the Berggasse ended in a flea market, a bustling square where all sorts of jumble was up for sale. The young doctor's wife would have much rather settled in a leafy residential suburb. She perhaps had something similar to Wandsbek in mind, a house with a garden and space for the children to play, rather like the houses where she would later pass the long summer holidays. Yet hard-working Sigmund relied upon being close to the university and having good access within the city.

The Freuds ended up living more than forty years in the Berggasse. It was here that Freud had his practice, together with the celebrated couch, a gift from a grateful patient.[3] In his room here, looking out into a Viennese courtyard with a great chestnut tree in it, Freud had some of the insights that were to make history. The rooms around him were filled with the commotion of family life. Professional and private life were closely contiguous. Little was to change in this respect throughout the course of the years. For the taste of the times, the furnishings of the flat – with its high ceilings, parquet flooring, damask wallpaper and homely tiled stoves – were neither modern nor avant-garde, but a respectable middle-class style characterized by solid comfort and a touch of distinction. Martha brought a certain amount with her from her family home, and the rest they bought as they went about turning their new lodgings into a home: beautiful furniture made from precious dark woods, comfortable plush chairs, magnificent oriental rugs, rich velvet portières, embroidered silk cushions, brilliant white crocheted covers, gleaming crystalware, delicate porcelain, more and more books, works of art, souvenirs, collectors' items, and framed photographs – a haven for the middle-class intellectual.

Daily life at Berggasse 19 was strictly regimented, its organization based upon a division of labour. Freud was soon made to realize this. Within just a few months of the wedding Martha was reprimanding him for disrupting the order she had imposed, to which he ironically replied that he probably had no option but to play the henpecked husband.[4] First-rate housewife that she was,[5] she tolerated neither carelessness nor slackness within her realm. Yet her methodical approach was just what Freud needed, for order, regularity and absolute punctuality were top priorities for both of them. Without the smooth running of the household, no one within it could have coped with the tasks at hand, least of all Freud: this smooth running was vital so that the view of the really important matters would not be obstructed. Trivialities were to remain just that. Freud was exempted from the 'hardships of life', as Martha put it, and could count on a domestic team capable of withstanding pressure. 'A good woman must be able to do everything', he used to say as an illustration of the high standards in the Freud household.[6] This not only involved everyone doing their best in their own particular field, but also helping create the special atmosphere they wanted their home to have. Oskar Pfister, a friend of the family, on one occasion told Martha how highly he regarded the family life that she had created and maintained, recalling his first visit to the Freuds in April 1909: 'In your house one felt as in a sunny spring garden, heard the gay song of larks and blackbirds, saw bright flower-beds, and had a premonition of the rich blessing of summer.'[7]

The Freud family enterprise, which looked so poetic from the outside, was managed by Martha with almost military rigour. Hardly a detail in the running of the household was left to chance. She organized and coordinated the housemaids in such a way that baths, stoves and breakfasts were prepared every bit as punctually as all the other tasks in the course of the day. Any decisions that were required on domestic matters were taken by Martha, and it was she who looked after the six children. Freud admitted that he had 'always let her have her way in the house'.[8] Her sovereignty within the family was beyond dispute. Responsibilities for supervising the children, running errands and carrying out other tasks were divided up between the housemaids, nursemaids and governesses, as well as Martha herself and later Minna. If guests came, there was always a spare place at table and drinks on hand. Everything worked like clockwork: the complexity of this unobtrusive and apparently automatic succession of daily duties remained a closed book to Freud and on one occasion prompted the doctor Ernst Simmel to comment drily that if he had a wife like Martha he too would have written all those books.

Early riser as he was, Freud is even said to have been given a helping hand in getting washed and dressed in the mornings. Martha had his clothes brushed and laid out ready for him, and rumour had it she would even put the toothpaste on his brush for him. At breakfast-time the whole family sat together. After a glance at the newspaper, they decided what had to be done and planned the day ahead. Duty called straightaway. The children had to go to school, Martha or one of the maids accompanying the youngest of them. Meanwhile, the first patients would be arriving. They were welcomed by a chambermaid, who would take their hat and coat and escort them to the waiting-room or straight to the professor. In the years of fame there would be a continuous stream of visitors to Berggasse 19, though the special partitioning of rooms and Freud's famously punctilious scheduling ensured that his patients rarely bumped into one another directly. Given the stir caused by his writings, many visitors may have expected to be confronted with an accomplished philanderer and bon vivant, yet they were received by a distinguished gentleman who took an active and unprejudiced interest in their own private world. The aura of the premises and the discretion and reserve of the much-respected professor in even the most sensitive of cases allowed patients to delve deeper into their past. Freud came across as sober, serious, objective, constantly attentive, sympathetic, forthcoming, and yet distant. His behaviour towards those seeking his advice was level-headed, trustworthy, honourable, and imbued with moral integrity: in short, it was the behaviour of a man of learning and decency. Martha was very much in the picture about who was visiting her husband at any particular time: she recognized the cars of prominent patients who drew up in front of the practice and knew who would get out.

Five minutes after the last patient had gone, the clock would strike one and it would be time for lunch. Even these small breaks and daily rituals were meticulously scheduled and followed a predictable routine.[9] The double door to the dining-room would open, and Martha and the six children would enter and take their seat at table. Freud would enter the room on the stroke of a gong, sitting down at the opposite end of the table to Martha. The maid would appear and start to serve the food. If one of the children was missing, Freud would briefly look at the empty seat before pointing at it silently with his knife or fork and giving his wife a quizzical glance – whereupon Martha would explain the whereabouts of the absent child. Taciturnity at table was nothing unusual. In general, Freud was silent when he ate. He often seemed lost in thought or would be closely studying some new acquisition from his collection of antiques, while later on his pains caused him trouble and made an ordeal of eating and talking. It was often Martha and the children who did the talking. Yet Freud always listened attentively to the stories recounted by his 'rabble': he and Martha followed with interest the progress made by the children and the adventures that befell them, taking pleasure in their successes and their enjoyment. This was something that remained particularly clearly etched in the family memory. Cases from the practice were not discussed at table, and there was no place for matters relating to psychoanalysis during family mealtimes – that is, unless they were entertaining some visitor from the field. To the general surprise of the guests, however, even then the head of the household was often monosyllabic and left the conversation to Martha and the children.[10]

From the point of view of the family, therefore, Freud kept his professional and private lives as separate as was permitted by the close spatial proximity of the two realms. Inside him, however, the one frequently merged with the other. Indeed, it was often day-to-day trivialities, incidents that Martha told him about, banal episodes from the children's lives, leftover scraps from dreams, tiny slips of the tongue, in other words things that were apparently unimportant or fortuitous, that provided the practical tools that helped him attain decisive insights into the apparatus of the mind and its complex functions. Yet there were limits to this, for Martha was vigorously opposed to any attempt to commandeer either herself or the children for the cause of psychoanalysis: the family was not to get caught up in such matters any more than was necessary. The fact that her husband often shut himself away in his rooms to work was congenial to this strategy. With Freud constantly going beyond limits anyway, she had to be all the firmer in setting them.

Following the lunch break, there was still some time for relaxation and a stroll round the block, which was also an opportunity to do a few local chores such as buying cigars or delivering a manuscript. Once the maids had served afternoon coffee at around four o'clock, it was back to work for all. Freud would receive more patients until it was time for the family supper, while Martha too still had things to do. She was on hand for the children, and would take them to visit families they were friendly with, or herself organize a social afternoon. It was not until the late evening, once the last patient had gone, the children were in bed, and Freud had managed to tear himself away from his desk (he would often write well into the night), that the two of them had some time to themselves. In these rare moments they would read or talk about this and that. When the opportunity arose, Martha and her husband would go for a late walk, frequently with Minna or one of the daughters, ending up at a café where they could have a chat or, in the summer, eat an ice-cream.[11]

At the weekends visits and activities were on the agenda. Occasionally they would go to galleries and museums; alternatively they would entertain friends and relatives, children and grandchildren. Even today Martha and Sigmund's grandchildren have fond memories of the hospitable atmosphere of the house and the regular visits they made to the Berggasse, when – as Anton W. Freud reported – the youngsters would appear wearing 'their best bib and tucker' and after the meal were generously provided with pocket money.[12] Anton's sister Sophie likewise described making visits of this sort accompanied by her nanny.[13] A regular fixture on Sundays, moreover, was the meal with Sigmund's mother Amalie. Within a rhythm of this sort, festival days came as a welcome change.

Even though the system of psychoanalysis was later seen by many as reminiscent of a sort of secular religion in which Freud played the role of pope, the atmosphere within the private sphere at least was a thoroughly worldly one. Important festivals were celebrated above all with the children in mind and without placing any stress on their religious background, and even this applied only to Christian holidays, not to Jewish ones: their son Martin had no memory of either himself or his brothers and sisters ever going to a synagogue. Though there were neither baptisms nor confirmations, they painted Easter eggs, decorated a Christmas tree each year, and had the traditionally sumptuous festive dinner of roast goose, candied fruits, cakes and punch.[14] Christmas was an opportunity for the family to be together and give one another presents. According to the Freuds' grandson Anton Walter, however, the main celebration and highlight of the year was the grandfather's birthday, when messages of congratulations would arrive from all over the world. Martha's birthday was celebrated following both the Jewish and the Christian calendar. Her official birthday in July fell in the long summer holidays, which the family as a rule spent away from the city. Wherever they happened to be staying in the summer, the Freuds would entertain just as many guests as they did in the Berggasse, and these would there and then form the 'party' to celebrate Martha's birthday. One nice custom of Martin's – his father spoke of *Dichteritis** or 'poetitis'[15] – was that whenever the occasion arose, and in particular on birthdays, he would compose a poem to be delivered to the person in question by one of the dogs.

The little private time they had was thus reserved predominantly for domestic diversions, family activities and a good deal of contact with like-minded friends. The opera, theatre and concerts were fairly infrequent pleasures for Sigmund and Martha – unless Yvette Guilbert happened to be performing – even though the moral conflicts and human tragedies of melodrama are rooted in a realm that is of particular relevance to the psychoanalyst.[16] Yet the few performances they did attend seem to have left all the more lasting an impression, and Freud's letters superbly re-create the emotions aroused by the events of the stage.[17] Music did not feature too prominently in the Freud family life. Neither Martha herself nor the children played an instrument, and Freud was completely unmusical, openly playing up his tone deafness and inability to carry a tune. As a child, indeed, when the young Freud's tender ears were disturbed by the piano études of one of his sisters, he convinced his parents that the instrument should vanish never to return,[18] and the same would have happened if half a dozen children armed with recorders, violins or pianos had raised the noise level unduly at Berggasse 19. Practising a musical instrument at home was scorned, and – as W. Ernest Freud recounted[19] – only Aunt Minna possessed a gramophone and a sizeable pile of crackling shellac records, which she enjoyed listening to every bit as much as the popular songs on the radio. In this way the sonorous voice of Enrico Caruso occasionally came to be heard in the Freud household, and Freud – who needed his peace and quiet and even had an aversion to the ringing of a telephone[20] – accordingly made sure that the whole contraption was banished to the farthest corner of the flat where it would bother him least.

---

*Translator's note: The German word playfully alludes to the *Diphteritis* or diphtheria that had almost killed his eldest daughter Mathilde when she was six. As Freud noted ironically in his *Jokes and their Relation to the Unconscious*, the coinage 'represents authorship by unqualified persons as another public danger'.

To help her cope with her many duties, Martha had a number of domestic servants who shared the tasks. For many years, the domestic staff – and more importantly the household – included a young Austrian woman called Paula Fichtl. It was in July 1929 that Paula first knocked at the Freuds' door to introduce herself, having come on the recommendation of her previous employer, the American Dorothy Tiffany Burlingham, who was the companion of Freud's daughter Anna. Mrs Burlingham also lived at Berggasse 19, one floor above them. Paula, who had worked for her as a nanny and was no longer needed in this capacity, was not exactly over the moon at her enforced change of circumstances and her new home. Her first thought was that she would 'have to do a lot of carpet-beating here',[21] and she feared it would be difficult working for the Freud family.[22] Yet she accepted the post and was introduced to her tasks as chambermaid by *Frau Professor*. To begin with she found the unwritten rules and regulations of the house, the tacit acceptance of the domestic routine, confusing and difficult to grasp. Though her new post was not quite as much of a jump in at the deep end as she had feared, she somehow felt she was not yet fully prepared for dealing with the Freud household. She compensated for her insecurity with zest and hard work and showed a clear determination to make herself indispensable.

The person she had most to do with was Martha. Her new employer struck her as a 'quiet woman' and as 'very particular about everything, like the real Hamburg woman she was'.[23] Everything had to be sparkling clean; not a speck of dust or fluff was to be tolerated anywhere. What brought them together, according to Paula, was the special affection they felt for the melancholy 'fairytale king' Ludwig II of Bavaria and their sympathetic interest in the fate of Empress Sisi, Elisabeth of Austria. Paula was very fond of *Frau Professor*, who did not look down upon her domestics but treated them with kindness and respect.[24] Martha's talent for organization, her constant self-discipline, her liking for neatness and tidiness, her thrift and circumspection, the virtues with which she attended to the affairs of everyday life, impressed Paula and rubbed off on her. For Paula, Frau Freud was in many respects an example to be followed. She was also 'the first friendly woman' in her life. Indeed, Paula was so attached to her that – whenever Martha was troubled by one of her severe migraines or other ailments – she would almost physically share her mistress's suffering. Martha 'knew how to manage servants', as her own son put it.[25] She was loved and respected by the rest of her domestic staff too. The surest testimony to Martha's agreeable nature and qualities of leadership was that her servants often remained with her for many years.

Paula Fichtl was a loyal servant and devoted her life entirely to her employers, coming to identify more and more with the Freud household and in many people's eyes actually becoming a part of it. She followed the Freuds when they emigrated and in the end became a sort of factotum around the house, sometimes more of a burden than a help.[26] Throughout the years she had an exalted sense of satisfaction at being in the service of a good and important household, and enjoyed her status in her own way. She treasured some of the letters she received, such as the charming one from the highly esteemed *Frau Prinzessin*, Princess Marie Bonaparte, as well as the kind words sent to her by David Astor, the owner and editor of *The Observer* newspaper. In 1980 she even received an official decoration, a medal of honour, for her help in establishing the Freud Museum and the 'special services' she had thereby rendered Austria.

Minna Bernays, Martha's Sister

Martha was supported in her labours not only by the domestic servants but, from the mid-1890s on, by her sister Minna (1865–1941) as well. The original plan was that she would stay at Berggasse 19 for just a few months. It ended up turning into a lifetime.

When her fiancé Ignaz Schönberg, a close friend of Freud's, died of tuberculosis in 1886, Minna first went to live with her mother in Hamburg-Wandsbek. She too had a legacy from her uncle, and she had also worked in various families as a governess or lady's companion. After Schönberg's death, she clearly came to terms with the idea of remaining unmarried and childless. 'She grew heavier, more jowly, becoming exceedingly plain', in the judge-

Minna Bernays

ment of Peter Gay.[27] Yet Minna developed other qualities and soon became an indispensable fixture of Berggasse 19. She too now had a family, and she and Martha were the 'two mothers' of the Freud children.[28] Within the family they apparently enjoyed similar rights, but this did not mean that the children were exposed to a double dose of maternal care and devotion. Rather, the responsibilities were divided up. In the case of Anna, who was the only one of the children to grow up practically from the outset in these new circumstances, this maternal division of labour did not have only positive effects. As the last-born child, she felt she was given a rather raw deal, with neither Martha nor Minna taking full responsibility for her needs.[29] Further, from Anna's point of view the new situation meant that along with her mother there was another woman who was the possible object of her father's affections, in other words another person with whom she was competing for her father's love.

For all the others, however, Minna's incorporation into the Freud family worked primarily to their advantage. Sigmund benefited considerably from her presence, and her familiarity with tarock – the card game he took such pleasure in – was just one of many reasons. Even during his engagement to Martha, he had recognized that his prospective sister-in-law, to whom he wrote affectionate letters, was not merely a discreet chaperon for intimate strolls with his sweetheart, but also a kindred spirit. He thought highly of her for her willingness, more than Martha, to face up to her mother, his adversary. In a letter to Martha, Freud perspicaciously contrasted the relation of the two daughters to their mother: 'You don't love her very much and are as considerate as possible to her; Minna loves her, but doesn't spare her.'[30] This difference between the two sisters in their relationship to the mother was important to Freud, and he used it cleverly.[31] He felt an affinity with Minna in their criticism of Emmeline and their endeavours to give the children a non-religious upbringing. On Saturdays Emmeline would chant Jewish prayers in her soft but steady, melodious voice, a ritual that disconcerted the Freud children.[32] Minna's secular outlook must have seemed like a breath of fresh air to Freud, aware as he was that in her heart of hearts Martha held to the spiritual legacy of her grandfather and the

Bernays family tradition. Yet the support his sister-in-law was to give him was more than just a matter of religion. Minna was a 'demilitarized zone' in the field of battle for family power.[33]

For Martha, too, the arrival of her sister was a boon, shifting the balance of power decisively when it came to family coalitions and providing her with an ally in the rebellion against Emmeline. Minna helped her free herself from her mother's rigid rule,[34] and possibly also promised protection from her demanding mother-in-law Amalie, who always kicked up something of a commotion with her energy and resolve, bursting on to the scene like a 'tornado'.[35] Though the two sisters were as thick as thieves and even seemed to some observers like 'Siamese twins',[36] they were by no means alike. Minna was strong, powerfully built, impressively self-confident and full of energy. Her character too was very different from Martha's and, as Freud once commented, more closely resembled his own, wild and passionate as she was. She came over as more vivacious and spontaneous than her elder sister, and was just as outspoken in her opinions as her mother. With her characteristically 'masculine' sharpness, she was the first in the ranks of androgynous intellectual women with whom Freud was to surround himself above all at the height of his fame. The more elegant Martha, by contrast, made a distinctly refined impression.[37]

Like Martha, Minna too had enjoyed a thorough education and was in many fields at least as knowledgeable as her sister, yet she also made a greater display of the intellectual side of her character. Even as a girl she was said to have constantly had her nose in a book, going about the tiresome business of housework with a duster in one hand and a book in the other.[38] Martha was different, sharp but rarely caustic; she was gentler, more delicate, quieter, more reticent, and all in all, as Freud said of her, the incarnation of his ideal of femininity. Martha seems not to have minded that her sister clearly had easier access to her husband and his sensitive profession. She left Minna to play the part of Freud's intellectual companion in this field, even at the risk that this might 'estrange' her from her husband.[39] Although he preferred women he could 'care for' and 'protect' (a 'robust female' was never his ideal),[40] the claim has even been made that Freud was unduly attracted to his sister-in-law, indeed that Minna was

The Freud family, 1898
In the garden at Berggasse 19
From left to right, from front to back:
Sophie, Anna, Ernst; Oliver, Martha Freud, Minna Bernays;
Martin, Sigmund Freud

'the secret love of Doctor Sigmund Freud'.[41] Yet this persistent rumour has been definitively dispatched to the land of cock-and-bull by Peter Gay.[42] The wildest of speculations were fired by the many journeys that brother- and sister-in-law undertook together, as well, perhaps, as details such as Minna's habit of occasionally answering the telephone with 'Frau Professor Freud'.[43] At least outwardly, Martha remained impervious to all doubt and untouched by the gossip. Whatever might have occurred behind the appearance of harmony and agreement, it evidently failed to create a rift between the sisters. Martha also went on journeys with her sister, as in 1923 when they visited the Tyrolean resort of Merano,[44] and claimed that there had 'never been any envy or discord between us'.[45]

The children, however, apparently did at times feel some degree of envy or jealousy at the collusion between mother and aunt and the virtual impossibility of playing them off against one another.[46] Significantly, for the last-born daughter at least, the family of Sigmund Freud, the discoverer of the Oedipus complex, was thus structured in such a way that the children, instead of fighting against the parent of the same sex to win the favour of the other, were faced with an alliance between two women who apparently succeeded in living in perfect harmony with one and the same man.

Sigmund and Martha Freud

'How intimate they were we will never know.'[47] This assessment by Appignanesi and Forrester provides a clue as to how much can ultimately be said about the phases following the emotional pyrotechnics of their stormy engagement. Both Sigmund and Martha kept their feelings for one another very much a private matter.[48] If to begin with it had looked as though Freud was well on the way to complete thraldom to his beloved, he was soon to let her know that, though the 'lyric phase' of their correspondence had come to a close with the wedding, Martha would now rediscover herself as a heroine in a new 'epic' form.[49]

Their relationship lasted a lifetime. There are said not to have been any violent arguments in the half-century of their partnership. The only row recorded in their fifty-three years of marriage was sparked by the question of the correct way of preparing cep mushrooms: with or without their stalks?[50] This unclouded connubial harmony might seem surprising – or, then again, perhaps not. After all, the terms of their union had been hammered out well in advance. As early as their engagement, the pattern their relationship was to follow had already begun to emerge. Freud demanded conformity and loyalty, and from the outset sought to mould Martha according to his wishes.[51] Martha resisted, opposing his attempts to impose his will, yet without renouncing her underlying peaceful disposition. If it could possibly be avoided, she would not cast the first stone. For Freud, attacking Martha was often like banging his head against a brick wall, which only served to make him even angrier. What he liked least was Martha's initial tendency to inhibit her aggressions or express them passively, her propensity to fight shy of conflicts and disputes, to hum and haw and fudge the issue instead of making it unequivocally clear where she stood.[52] Her stonewalling was capable of driving Freud to distraction. He preferred having things out, even when this proved painful. When had he ever shirked unpleasantness or buried his head in the sand?

On the other hand, Martha's diplomatic strategies also allowed him to see her in a special light: Martha, he felt, was one of those people who were kind-hearted by their very nature and whose goodness was inherited, while others – himself included – only reached this higher stage after fierce inner conflicts. Freud thus found that Martha had more than just 'human happiness' to offer him:[53] he had much reason to be grateful to her, and would die in her debt. In his eyes, perhaps, she embodied a better world, or perhaps a better sort of person or the hope of one. It seems he saw in his wife an almost celestial being who protected him from 'any kind of meanness', and it took him greatly by surprise when she once admitted that at times she had to suppress bad or evil thoughts.[54]

Yet his angel was on one occasion not far from expelling him from his paradise. One of her letters made it clear to him that, temporarily at least, she had inwardly distanced herself from him.[55] This realization provoked deep insecurity and anxiety in Freud. Yet it did not damage his underlying feelings towards her. As long as Martha protected him from meanness, he was exempted from feeling that way himself, however 'bad' the thoughts he might entertain. One problem was the incompatibility between his desire to embrace Martha's goodness himself and the almost equally powerful aspiration to bring her to share his feelings of aggression, hostility, hatred and irreconcilability, as was the case in his clash with Eli. As we know, Martha generally refused to countenance Freud's belligerence, but this in turn fuelled further doubts. The question was the reason for her evasiveness. Was it weakness and cowardice? Inwardly, this could only have met with his disdain. Or was it really her innate goodness and sweet temper? Then he would have no option but to throw himself at her feet, so to speak. He often wavered between the two possibilities, but in the long run it was the second that gained the upper hand. Quite simply, Martha was noble by nature. Previously it had tended to be virtues such as discipline, ambition, drive and willpower that had featured in his life rather than qualities such as love, sympathy or the facility for dialogue.[56] But the latter were the aptitudes that mattered in his relation to Martha, and here she had the advantage. More than her husband, Martha succeeded in using her capacity for empathy as a way of overcoming hurdles. Sigmund, by contrast, was often lacking in tact and sensitivity.

His tone, as recorded in the letters, could at times come across as rather condescending. His mild, forbearing manner was that of a man who did not hold her ignorance and simple-mindedness against her – for she was fortunately so reasonable in other respects! It seems he took it for granted that he would emerge victorious from whatever game they played. In this way, Martha would be a constant reminder of his greatness and superiority. At the same time, however, she was not to be too meek. He wanted to goad her into opposition, to provoke her, in order then to lavish her with affection: 'It wasn't so bad, after all', he wrote to her, 'to read something every month that came from the depths of passion. When you are mine we must have a little quarrel at least once a week, so that your love can always start fresh again.'[57] Martha proved willing to oblige.

It was not long before this relationship of 'authority and submission'[58] was running smoothly. Martha recognized that her husband was always particularly tender and compliant after one of his outbursts. She knew how to cope with his swings of mood, and was generally prepared to put up with them. In personal terms she was well equipped to do so. The loss of her father a few years prior to her engagement, which had left her in the broadest sense unprotected, in conjunction with the domineering character of her mother, which she found difficult to oppose, may well have fostered her skills and heightened her tolerance in this respect. Yet on at least one occasion she came close to giving up. She found it more difficult than she had hoped to come to terms with the many – perhaps too many – changes that Freud demanded she make, and with the expectations he had of her, which she was so keen to fulfil. In such moments she quite seriously doubted whether she was worthy of being his wife.[59] The conflict came to a head whenever Freud asked something unreasonable or expected the impossible of her. On such occasions she had to muster all her diplomatic skill to defuse embarrassing and unpleasant situations.[60] Freud had a rather different view of matters and would often say that his wife had only two duties in life, to keep well and to love him.[61] Though indeed attracted to beautiful, fashionable and narcissistic women,[62] he did not want an egocentric prima donna as his partner. Perhaps influenced by the example of capricious Amalie, he suspected that it would not be easy to live with someone self-centred or fickle. It may well, therefore, have been some sort of flight from the moodiness of his demanding mother that led him to gentle Martha, a woman who promised to keep good control of her emotions and yet idolized him as his mother had. For Freud it was clear that 'finding a respected name and a warm atmosphere in her home was decisive in my choice of a wife'.[63] His noble 'little princess' was to turn into a loving wife on whose affection he could count.

What had become of the fascination that Martha had exerted on her sweetheart in the early days? One thing that is certain is that the relentless incursion of day-to-day reality took its toll. Time together was always in short supply. Freud worked unflaggingly receiving patients and followers of his ideas, who would have commandeered him round the clock if they could have, and took up all his energy as it was. For long periods of time, Freud was but a ghostly half-presence at home, busy at work in the remotest rooms of their spacious flat.

Their silver wedding anniversary in September 1911, which they celebrated in family circles in Klobenstein in the Dolomites, was an occasion to look back on the past. What must the two of them have been thinking as they cast their mind back on that April day twenty-nine years earlier when they had first met? More than a quarter of a century had passed since then, turbulent times with their ups and downs. The seeds they had sown had borne fruit; the crop had been a rich one. But what did their life together still have in store for them? By the ten years prior to Freud's death, when old age and illness were leaving their mark, the priorities in the relation of husband and wife had clearly shifted.[64] Martha's position at her husband's side was incontestable, and for this reason he no longer needed to give special prominence to how much she meant to him. But was there a cloud hanging over their relationship, something they did their best to conceal from the world at large? As Ronald Clark wrote, 'during the 1930s there was even slight irritation – well controlled as Freud's reactions always were – and it seemed that there was little left of the earlier great love.'[65]

The golden anniversary in September 1936, which the diaries tersely record with the entry '50th wedding anniversary', was celebrated in Vienna with a sunny reception in the garden, numerous visitors coming to pay their respects with flowers and presents. One novelty was that the festivities were filmed by Ruth Mack Brunswick, a friend from psychoanalytical circles.[66] The film shows an elderly couple, serene and tranquil. After all their years together, they had nothing more to prove, nothing more to question, no reason to change the way things were arranged. The future had become shorter.

In all their years of marriage hardly a complaint had passed Martha's lips. Although herself astonishingly active, she did without a good many things that were no longer possible for Sigmund, such as trips together to visit the children, out of a sense of solidarity and supportiveness. Her husband, who in 1912 had told his future son-in-law Max Halberstadt[67] that he had 'really got along very well' with his wife and was thankful to her 'for the children who have turned out so well, and for the fact that she has neither been very abnormal nor very often ill', gauged their marriage by its results: children, health, affection. In a letter to his eldest daughter Mathilde he described what 'the more intelligent among young men' look for in a wife: 'gentleness, cheerfulness, and the talent to make their life easier and more beautiful'.[68] Speaking of his wife in 1936, he said: 'It was really not a bad solution of the marriage problem, and she is still today tender, healthy, and active.'[69] Even at an early stage in their relationship, he had anticipated that Martha would be 'an adored sweetheart in youth, and a beloved wife in maturity'.[70] He had prophesied that she would understand 'that even for a beloved girl there is still one further step up: to that of friend'.[71]

Travel

On his return from Paris in 1886, Freud had assured his fiancée he wanted to marry her as soon as possible: 'then together we could practise the skill in travelling which I have acquired during the past seven months.'[72] Yet this promise of Freud's was to remain largely unfulfilled. Although he did take comparatively long annual breaks away from the Berggasse, this time was not devoted solely to his wife and family. The travel habits of the Freud family displayed a number of unusual features, above all the fact that they did not spend all their holiday together. For many years, after a few weeks of harmonious country life in the Austrian mountains or on the North Italian lakes, Freud would head off on his own for the south.[73] Such was the custom, albeit not from the outset.

In the first years of marriage, with the horde of children constantly on the increase, plans for the summer months were none too ambitious, and the Freuds were happy to settle for destinations not far from Vienna. What Martha and Sigmund were after was a health resort in rural surroundings, some two to three hours away by train, and offering good air and a pleasant landscape. The young couple spent August 1888, the summer after the birth of their first child, in the village of Maria Schutz on the Semmering. This magnificent mountain resort had a reputation as a popular haunt of the monarchy, and high society and the nobility used to come here in pursuit of distraction. Popular as it was, the area had been rapidly developed and was easily accessible, just the job for a relaxing holiday. This was the Freuds' favourite destination until the mid-1890s.[74] From nearby Reichenau Sigmund wrote, 'I do not think I can get Martha away from here anymore'.[75] The Freuds were the sort of people who preferred to pitch camp in places that were already familiar to them, but were also receptive to new ideas. The base where they were staying would always be the point of departure for extended excursions and further explorations of the surrounding area.

In the late 1890s they spent several summers at Bad Aussee in Styria. In 1899 they opted for Berchtesgaden in Bavaria, where Freud wrote *The Interpretation of Dreams*, and they were to visit Berchtesgaden and the Königsee on several more occasions at the

At Altaussee, 1905
Martha Freud with her husband and mother-in-law

beginning of the new century. After this, Lavarone in North Italy became their family holiday destination, and it was from here that in 1906 they made an excursion to Lake Garda in two horse-drawn carriages. For their son Martin, this dusty gallop down steep, winding lanes, past lush vineyards and through picturesque villages, was the most beautiful journey he ever made.[76] Martha and Sigmund were to be drawn back again to such pleasant holiday resorts as Lavarone.

As the children grew up, the Freuds' summer plans changed in character. The requirements of health and what Freud referred to as 'the whims of old age' started to make themselves felt, and Sigmund and Martha came to lay the emphasis on recuperation and gathering new strength. In 1910 and the following years, as well as during the First World War, they thus spent restful weeks in the fashionable city of Karlsbad. Friends now played an increasingly important part in their travel programmes, both as companions and welcome guests and also helping them out where necessary. Sándor Ferenczi proved to be one such friend, making it possible for the Freuds to take a holiday in the difficult summers of 1917 and 1918 by getting in contact with Hungarian friends who owned summer houses in Csorbató. The circumstances dictated what was feasible. During the war years the Freud family preferred cities such as Salzburg, where the infrastructure was in a better state than in more remote regions.[77]

In the early 1920s, when the children were grown up and Freud had been diagnosed as having cancer, the range of possible destinations shrunk further. As a rule the Freuds remained within Austria, again heading for the Semmering more often. By the 1930s Freud had come to depend totally on being close to his doctors, and he and Martha would spend the summers in the green belt around Vienna, where they would rent a spacious villa with a garden. They spent the summers of 1931 and 1932 in Poetzleinsdorf and in 1933 opted for Unterdöbling. During this holiday they became especially aware of the changes that were going on at the time. Just a few days after arriving at their summer quarters, they learnt of the burning of the books in front of the Berlin Opera House, where – to the accompaniment of bands playing music and torchlight parades – thousands of 'un-German' books blacklisted by the Nazis had been committed to the flames. Along with the works of other unacceptable authors, Freud's writings burnt here too. Freud commented laconically on the vile spectacle: in the Middle Ages, he said, they would have burnt him, whereas nowadays they made do with burning his books – progress indeed! This 'progress' signalled his final years in Austria. The summers of 1934 and 1937, spent in their holiday home in the Strassergasse, were to be their last there.

The Freuds' annual departure for several weeks of summer holidays was a time-consuming business. Many years the enterprise was more or less akin to a complete removal and required due preparation. Often the first reconnaissance work would be carried out around Easter time, generally by Sigmund and his brother Alexander. It was sometimes not easy finding the right location, and Martha found it surprising given her husband's fame that the problem could not simply be solved by means of a generous benefactor.[78] The search for accommodation was always a serious matter, with nothing to be left to chance.

As the holiday period approached, Martha took all the necessary measures. As in most families from bourgeois circles, mother and children departed at the beginning of summer, while Sigmund – who was kept at home by the call of duty – would follow at a later date. Ever thinking of her husband's welfare, Martha would make sure that her grass widower did not fall into rack and ruin. The few bottles of 'heavenly marsala' he was intending to indulge in one year were to be enjoyed at most 'in drops': 'Martha counted the bottles and took charge of them lest in my loneliness I succumb to the consolation of drink.'[79] At all events, Martha was on her guard: after all, these were weeks in which he was only too prone to call on his sweet 'Friend Marsala for help'[80] or seek 'restoration in a bottle of barolo'.[81]

The next job to be done was to convey the horde of children with all their paraphernalia safe and sound to their destination, which was anything but easy. Even the rail journey was an adventure. Martin Freud never ceased to wonder at his mother's masterly logistical achievements.[82] Under her supervision the family pulled off the feat of fitting six excited children, a couple of servants and a whole host of unwieldy luggage into a cramped third-class train compartment, using cushions and blankets to turn the spartan wooden benches into reasonably comfortable and even rather homely quarters – without it all degenerating into pure pandemonium. If need be, Martha would hang a hammock across the compartment and unceremoniously put one of the children up on high. All the while she would be calmly supervising the maids, never losing track of what was going on, never missing a trick or forgetting a detail. She planned, calculated, guided and carried out the seemingly impossible. Martha knew that this travelling arrangement – a battle she knew she would win – would have been 'torture' for her husband. According to Martin, she did not give him the choice of exposing himself to this strain, and he was doubtless happy to comply. In her discreet way she made it possible for him to make the journey 'alone and in comfort'.[83]

Freud's arrival at their holiday accommodation was always the high point of the year. Now the children had their father all to themselves for a few weeks. Together they roamed through the woods on overgrown paths, looked for mushrooms, gathered berries, or went boating, fishing or swimming. Once home, Martha would clean the generally abundant harvest of mushrooms, and the question of what the cook would prepare for dinner was resolved once more. Like other women, Martha frequently stayed away from the expeditions across fields and meadows, and tried to relax in her own way, enjoying the peace and quiet and going for strolls along well-trodden paths.[84] For a long time Freud believed she did not even know how to 'climb' and did not feel at ease in the mountains, until on one occasion she impressed him with a notable ascent.[85] Typical of Martha and of the time was that even in the isolation of their holiday resorts she took care to wear correct clothing. While her husband swapped his suits made from English cloth for a pair of good old-fashioned knickerbockers, and the children went around in indestructible lederhosen or dirndls,[86] it was impossible to imagine Martha in anything like trousers, a pullover or sandals. This was simply a question of style. Even on the hottest of days and unobserved by strangers, she would never have dressed in more risqué or casual fashion. She was a lady, and as such would not do without her long skirts, collars and stays.[87] Any kind of informality was foreign to her, both when she was herself still quite young and later, when the prevailing customs as regards the way people dressed were becoming more lax.[88]

From the mid-1890s onwards there was a gradual change in the tried and tested family summer holiday arrangements. Throughout September 1895 Martha, who was expecting their sixth child, had expressed a desire to go on a journey together with her husband – perhaps like the year before when, at her suggestion, after spending a few weeks with the children, they had been to Lovran on the Adriatic with Minna.[89] Prior to this, all they had managed was a week at Hallstadt and Bad Aussee in 1892 and the odd trip to meet up with friends, as in 1894 when they had joined Wilhelm Fliess and his wife in Munich. Yet it was not until two years later, in August 1897, that Sigmund and Martha headed abroad on the first holiday the two of them had taken together without the children since their honeymoon. Their destination was Venice, Tuscany and Umbria.[90] In a letter to Fliess he described with an undertone of mild irritation the difficulties he was having fixing the dates for this journey: allowances had to be made, for example, for Martha's 'indisposition'.[91] On later occasions, too, their joint travel adventures seemed ill-fated. On the second major trip with Martha, to Dalmatia and North Italy in August 1898, he had to leave her behind in Ragusa (modern-day Dubrovnik) on account of a stomach upset – possibly a welcome excuse for her to spare herself the exertions of the rest of the journey. Other years she only joined her husband for certain stages of their holiday.[92] September 1900 was the last time for many years that Freud was to travel alone with Martha, from then on making his trips in the trusted company of his brother Alexander, Minna or some other like-minded colleague.[93]

The choice of new travel companions was not the only change. Something else Martha had to confront was that her husband was loosing certain inner bonds, a development that manifested itself in his passion, long repressed, for southern landscapes and culture. In the long run, his rural holidays with the family were no longer enough for him. He did not make a complete break, however. Instead he transformed his country walks into material for his work. His passion for mushrooms, for example, prompted comparisons with the navel of a dream, the point where it reaches down into the unknown and spreads into an intricate network. Everything he experienced left its mark on ideas, visions and linguistic metaphors. Travel impressions too provided him with intellectual nourishment, and he wanted more. Usually towards the end of the summer, therefore, Freud would bid his family farewell and set off on an educational journey. The time of year in which the heat gradually abated was his alone.

If material constraints and questions of expediency had initially been decisive in prompting Freud's solitary travels[94] – since long, costly voyages with wife and children hardly seemed practicable, while sight-seeing marathons were certainly not suitable holidays for small children – other arguments can be brought to bear for the years when their outward circumstances had changed. Martha in particular, and Sigmund too, was not especially interested in taking all their holidays together. For a start, Martha continued to be tied down by her duties to the children and in the home, even though Freud's sister Rosa and the nannies took some of the load.[95] Secondly, as Ernest Jones reported, she did not have too much time for the passion – or rather the restlessness – with which her husband obsessively indulged his scientific interests even when travelling. She preferred to spend just part of the holidays with her husband and to enjoy this time all the more fully. She was neither willing nor able to keep up with the pace as he positively scoured the sights and museums. While she took things in at her leisure, her husband's ideal was to sleep 'in a different bed each night'.[96] Martha was happy to leave such whirlwind tours to him and on occasion even persuaded him to make certain trips on his own.[97] Without her, he clearly got his money's worth.

There was no stopping him, especially once he had overcome his fear of travelling,[98] his intense fear of train journeys in particular, and of arriving at certain destinations – in a metaphorical sense, as well. As a result of this anxiety neurosis, for a long time Freud could only visit many of the places he was drawn to in his imagination or by following his finger on the map. The Eternal City was a central focus of this wanderlust. In a letter to Wilhelm Fliess he wrote that his yearning for Rome was becoming 'ever more tormenting'.[99] Around 1900, when publication of the epoch-making *The Interpretation of Dreams* failed to provoke the storms of enthusiasm he was hoping for, a disappointed Freud felt lonely, unappreciated and frustrated. For months his spirits were low, as can hardly have escaped Martha's notice. Doubtless guessing the reasons for his discontentment, she even made occasional suggestions about who to send his *Dream Book* to.[100] Her husband tried to come to terms himself with what was going on inside him, and it was his constant self-analysis that gave him the boost he needed. When the time was ripe, he succeeded in shaking off his doubts and reservations, and decided to take the bull by the horns. In September 1901 he finally set off for Rome, a feat of personal bravura and a 'high point', as he put it, in his life.[101] The world had become his oyster.

The first journey to Rome broke the shackles that had held him back before, and there was nothing now to stop him making further trips. Future summers saw him restlessly making his way from place to place, finding stimulation for his work wherever he went. Artefacts from the past shaped his ideas. He passionately collected antique statuettes, vases and wall decorations. He surrounded himself with these acquisitions in his study and even used his exhibits to test his theories, asking himself what drives the people of earlier cultures were moved by and how they manifested themselves, what the constantly recurring questions were, and whether there was possibly some sort of leitmotif running through human history. Time and again, his figurines proved suitable guides for digging into archaic terrain. In these cultural artefacts that silently spoke of our forefathers' knowledge of the world, the culture of the present disclosed itself to Freud, who recognized the remarkable analogy between archaeology and psychoanalysis:[102] with each layer that is meticulously removed an earlier one comes to light, the aim being to venture into the depths so as to unearth the origins and perhaps the 'truth'. These were the impulses that drove him to undertake his voyages of discovery and immerse himself in the distant past.

A rapid succession of letters and postcards allowed his wife and children to share in his enduring – and indeed overwhelming – impressions. He promised to make up for the many brief written communications with an exhaustive account in person. It meant a great deal to Freud to keep in constant contact with his family.[103]

The energy he derived from his Rome experiences spurred him to tie up the professorship to which he aspired, which was at the time still hanging in the balance. To this end he set about enlisting the support of influential contacts such as his former patient Elise Gomperz, whose husband had earlier commissioned the young Freud to translate a number of essays by John Stuart Mill. At first it was to no avail. It was another grateful patient, Baroness Ferstel, who finally succeeded in eliciting from the minister responsible the promise that Freud would be promoted, making her 'request' seem more appealing with the gift of a painting by Emil Orlik that the minister had his eye on for the gallery he was planning to set up.[104] Her obliging efforts bore fruit, and Freud was given his title in February 1902. It was a great moment for the whole family. Martha was delighted at the long overdue official recognition of her husband and proud to be able to call herself *Frau Professor*. Buoyed by the academic support, Freud began consciously enlisting followers, and in autumn 1902 set up a regular meeting of disciples of psychoanalysis at Berggasse 19. The Wednesday Society was to become the nucleus of the psychoanalytical movement.[105]

After his numerous explorations of Europe at the beginning of the century, Freud's world shrunk with the onset of cancer. The physical suffering caused by the sequence of painful operations and treatments to which he was subjected closed the door to the south he so loved. From 1923 it was once again home pastures that provided the backdrop for the diversions of the summer. Freud was more dependent than ever on Martha, who soon had to assume even greater responsibility for all the organization. In mid-May 1930 Martha travelled to Carinthia to look for their summer accommodation, a task that her husband had previously been happy to take on himself. She decided upon a house at Rebenburg on the Grundlsee,[106] and it was here that Freud learnt that he had been awarded the Goethe Prize. 'And so', he wrote to his family, 'thanks to Mama's energy we have a summer residence.'[107] This reconnaissance trip was not the first journey Martha had undertaken alone or without her husband. As a young woman she had already shown herself a keen traveller,[108] and after the exhausting pregnancy and birth of their last child she had tried to pick up where she had left off before. This time she had not recovered as quickly as previously and, enervated and worn out as she was, she urgently needed rest and a bit of distance. In 1896 she took her first holiday alone since their wedding ten years before,[109] spending two weeks with her mother in Hamburg and stopping off in Berlin to visit the Fliess family on the way back.

Berlin

In the years after the turn of the century Berlin assumed a special significance for the Freuds, emerging alongside Vienna as the 'family headquarters'.[110] From being little more than a seat of royalty, the vibrant German capital had blossomed into a hub of cosmopolitanism and a Mecca for science. There developed an unparalleled concentration of scholars, artists and intellectuals of all orientations, which in turn further fostered the city's image. The Freuds too succumbed to the fascination exerted by Berlin. Sigmund even considered moving there.[111] As early as 1874 he had intended to spend the winter semester in Berlin[112] and later, following his months with Charcot, he had been a guest student at the university: after being there a week he had still not seen a great deal, but resolved 'at least to go to the aquarium in the near future'. He found Berlin more sober than Paris and 'somewhat less pretty' than Vienna. 'Life is much cheaper', he told Martha, 'people slave harder, a lot of constables and soldiers. In a house on Unter den Linden – not even a very splendid one – with a pretty flag fluttering from it, lives the ancient Kaiser, who currently has a cold again.'[113] Shortly afterwards he spoke of a visit to the 'Court Hairdresser', the best barber in town, as well as planned trips to the theatre and calls paid to the Café Bauer.[114]

Besides the first, fleeting impressions, however, there were other, weightier reasons for Freud's weakness for Berlin: it was here that Freud's work found broad and serious recognition in the early days. It was in Berlin that Karl Abraham, who had worked for three years under the directorship of Carl Jung at the Burghölzli psychiatric clinic near Zurich and had come under Freud's influence at the age of thirty in 1907, founded the first – and for some years only – private psychoanalytic practice in Germany.[115] With a grand total of five members, including the contentious sexologist Magnus Hirschfeld, the enterprising neurologist Abraham in 1908 brought into being the Berlin Psychoanalytic Society, the nucleus of the Berlin Branch Society of the International Psychoanalytic Association founded in 1910 at the International Congress of Psychoanalysts in Nuremberg. He later became a leading training analyst. The commitment shown by the Berlin doctors under Abraham's influence turned the city into one of the centres of world psychoanalysis. The first psychoanalytical sanatorium, Schloss Tegel, was also located here.[116] Set in beautiful surroundings – the path leading to Schloss Tegel passed via Spandau through a pine wood and along the River Havel – the clinic itself was surrounded by a sprawling park with inviting benches and a glass-covered pavilion. The sanatorium opened its gates in April 1927 under the directorship of Ernst Simmel. Together with Max Eitingon, Simmel had in 1920 founded the Berlin Policlinic, an outpatient clinic 'for the psychoanalytic treatment of nervous ailments', with an affiliated training institute as well. Over the following years he had struggled in vain to find public sponsors for a clinic run along psychoanalytical lines: it was only the involvement of prominent partners from Vienna and Berlin that enabled the project to be set up and run as a private enterprise.[117] Freud's son Ernst, an architect, designed the interior of the building. A model of its kind, the sanatorium had facilities for treating between twenty-five and thirty patients, frequently with chronic psychoneurotic and somatic complaints, and in particular addicts. The original plans also included a self-contained department for cases of psychosis, but this was vetoed by the von Heinz family, who owned the main castle.[118]

Freud took a fond interest in the intense activities of the Berliners and the development of their institutions, and on several occasions between 1928 and 1930 stayed at the castle when he was in Berlin having a new prosthesis fitted by Professor Schröder.[119] Yet in spite of all efforts and the outstanding work that was done there, this pioneering psychoanalytic institution was battling against ruin. By March 1930 bankruptcy was imminent. Ernst Simmel issued an appeal to the Prussian Minister of Culture, asking for above all moral support in the setting up of a foundation that would ensure the clinic's survival.[120] The sum raised by an appeal for donations in 1929, which also included contributions from friends of the Freud family such as Dorothy Burlingham and Marie Bonaparte, was not enough. The upkeep and above all the personnel costs were too high. By August 1931 it was no longer possible to pay the rent, and the clinic had to close down.

Yet this by no means meant the end of the Berlin connection for the Freuds. There were many private links, too. Freud's sons as well as other members and friends of the family had succumbed to the pull of the German capital – grounds enough for an occasional trip to Berlin. Martha in particular took advantage of the opportunity, especially as the journeys could conveniently be combined with a trip home to Hamburg, as was the case in February 1900,

Schloss Tegel sanatorium

when her mother turned seventy. Martha fostered many contacts in Berlin and also visited the hospitable Abraham family, with whom the Freuds had long been on the closest of terms.[121] In May 1908, Sigmund Freud told his colleague in Berlin: 'My wife has reported to me a great deal about the cordial reception she found at your house.'[122]

Freud's family and relatives also met one another in the city. When Max Halberstadt was in Berlin on business in June 1930, he stayed with his brother-in-law Ernst.[123] Martin visited his brothers and their families here and also met up with his old friend Hans Lampl and his wife Jeanne.[124] Over the years, there were more and more occasions for such visits, and at times they caused feelings to run high. This was the case, for example, at Christmas 1926, when the Freuds travelled to Berlin to spend the festive days with the families of Ernst and Oliver, including three grandchildren whom the grandparents had not yet met. It was a trip that provoked intense jealousy in Anna, who had to stay at home with an injured foot.[125] Time and again, she felt, she had shelved her own activities in order to be with her ailing father, yet no sooner had he suddenly regained his taste for adventure, than off he went without so much as a by your leave. It upset her greatly that he

In the park at Schloss Tegel
From left to right: Ernst Simmel, Anna and Sigmund Freud,
Moshe Wulff and his wife

could get by without her active support and could be cared for well enough by his wife on her own.

This was not the first time that the old rivalry between mother and daughter had produced such touchiness. The Berlin trips of these years repeatedly sparked a contest for the place at Freud's side. In 1929, for example, when Freud was planning a two-week stay at the Tegel sanatorium, Anna went to great trouble re-arranging and cancelling her own work commitments so as to be able to accompany him. She protested vigorously against Martha travelling with him, and behaved like a suitor jealously competing for the affection of a lover: 'At first Mama wanted to go in my place', she wrote, 'but I did not want that at all.'[126] Anna insisted on her place at Freud's side, with no consideration for the feelings of her mother.[127]

Following her own earlier experiences with Sigmund, however, Martha was forearmed against claims to absolute rights and out-bursts of petty jealousy, and showed herself unwilling to yield. She had long since acquired a taste for going visiting and had no intention of giving it up. So it was at the end of March 1930.[128]

Freud had been planning to go to Berlin for a refitting of his prosthesis, a monstrous contraption designed to replace teeth and parts
of his mouth that had been infected by cancer. Martha was to
accompany him. Yet as the prosthetic device – which had never
really fitted perfectly – was unexpectedly bearable at the time,
Freud postponed his visit to the capital. Martha, meanwhile, kept
to their original travel plans and departed for Berlin for the thirty-
eighth birthday of their son Ernst, stopping off briefly in Prague as
well.[129] She helped with the preparations, stayed in a comfortable
hotel,[130] and enjoyed her days there. Her husband was delighted
to see her indulging herself in this way: 'I am very pleased you kept
your good room in the hotel', he wrote. 'We are too old to save
money.' He closed his letter warmly with the words: 'Have your-
self "a good time", as they say in America.'[131] And she did. She led
an active social life during her stay,[132] was out and about almost
more than she otherwise was in Vienna, and took an unusual interest in the psychoanalytic business. She paid a visit not only to
Eitingon and his wife Mirra at their house in the Altensteinstrasse
in Berlin-Dahlem, but the next day even went to the Berlin
Psychoanalytical Institute in the Wichmannstrasse. Her husband
was baffled to learn of her exploits: 'It was with respect and
admiration that I heard and read of your social achievements in
Berlin. I will not be imitating you.'[133] Martha returned to Vienna
in 'the best of moods, very content with her Berlin impressions and
experiences'.[134]

In the following years too, as illness dictated her husband's way
of life, Martha continued to travel alone, visiting the family as well
as friends from psychoanalytical circles.[135] As on her previous
trips to Berlin, in 1932 she again opted for comfortable accommodation that offered her peace and quiet and the chance to be
alone, especially since her son Ernst's flat was on the fourth floor
and rather inconvenient for his seventy-year-old mother.[136] This
time her stay in Berlin was shadowed by the disaster to come. The
economic slump and the political menace unsettled Martha profoundly, and she told Freud of her fears.[137] Freud shared her
worries and the scepticism with which she viewed what lay ahead:
'The times are actually awfully bad and totally without any gua-
rantee of a bearable future.'[138] Martha was not mistaken in the

dark forebodings she had in Berlin, yet at this point neither she nor the rest of the family suspected just how far their life would shortly be thrown into turmoil and how momentous the consequences would be. The Freuds who lived in Berlin had felt at ease in their adopted home, and loved the city. It was with extreme bewilderment that they came to view themselves as outsiders and scapegoats in surroundings that were still so familiar to them. Their Jewishness, which had played but a minor part in their upbringing, had suddenly become a matter of vital importance. They had no choice but to start looking for a new place to live.

Friends

The social life of the Freud family was far-reaching in its scope. Organizing it was the responsibility of the housewife.[139] They often had guests at Berggasse 19, though only rarely did they throw a party. They had little time for glittering balls or wild celebrations. It was something more like the spirit of an intellectual salon that prevailed in the Berggasse.

One favourite ritual was the weekend game of tarock, a habit that was kept up for many years. The players often staged their tarock evenings at Freud's house, where Martha ensured that the setting was right and provided the assembled gentlemen – who included colleagues such as Oscar Rie, Leopold Königstein, Ludwig Rosenberg, and later on occasionally the Freuds' son Martin – with a few titbits that would pleasantly enhance their powers of endurance.[140]

Another regular at-home that established itself at Berggasse 19 was the Wednesday Psychological Society. The true nucleus of the psychoanalytical movement,[141] the Wednesday Society was a group of men who, on invitation by postcard, met regularly on Wednesday evenings in Freud's waiting-room. Martha provided cakes, red wine and black coffee, while Freud took care of the tobacco. Ashtrays were distributed all over the table, one for each cigar-smoking guest. In the heat of the moment, the scientific exchanges grew more and more stimulating, the clouds of smoke ever thicker, and the evenings longer. Inspired by their discussions, when the time came to part company they would often decide to have one more for the road together somewhere,[142] keeping their train of thought going with what was definitely the final cigar and possibly the final drink. With a touch of humour they dedicated the first session of the Wednesday Society to the psychology of smoking.

Most of the Freuds' long-standing friends came from the same academic milieu or had come into contact with Freud through professional channels. It was customary for the ladies – often doctors' wives like Martha – to invite one another over on a regular basis. If Martha's friends were visiting, Sigmund would usually limit himself to looking in briefly or joining them for a few minutes if the guests included anyone of interest to him. Otherwise he would leave them to their own devices. As it was, he was not equally taken with all of Martha's friends. On one occasion he had been particularly antagonized by her friendship with a certain Elise, a girl who had 'married before her wedding' and had a child out of wedlock.[143] Martha, whose moral views were based on a sense of responsibility towards other people, showed herself understanding towards Elise,[144] while Freud showed no mercy and forbade his then fiancée all contact with her. Although he appreciated that Martha had shown herself not to be 'prudish', he sneered that decency 'doesn't seem to worry Elise' and scoffed in particular at her 'utter weakness and lack of principle'.[145] He was also worried about their good standing, for 'what one of us does will also be charged to the other's account'. Martha objected that her own impeccable reputation made it perfectly acceptable for her to associate with Elise.

Other social connections were more to his taste, and also more useful. At intervals Martha would pay official visits to the wives of Freud's close friends and his Viennese followers.[146] The psychoanalytical movement formed a family, and the family was part of the movement. With her calm and friendly manner, the Hamburg-born *Frau Professor* found it easy to make contacts, even though she at first struck strangers as reserved and it took a while to get close to her. To begin with, she came over as rather distant, proud, reticent and shy, and rarely showed her feelings.[147] Yet once she was on more intimate terms with a person, she proved an understanding and warm-hearted friend who could always be counted on.[148] She took pleasure in looking after visitors from abroad. She made sure that any such visitors – and in particular the women – were given a good reception in Vienna, inviting them round for chats and helping them look for a flat or get hold of tickets for the theatre or concerts.[149] The ladies of the house, and especially Martha, would show their guests round Vienna, and take them to art collections, cafés, bookshops and antiquarian booksellers. 'They were delightful days', as one grateful visitor summarized the Freuds' personalized tourist programme.[150]

The Freuds were very accommodating hosts, even though certain visitors to Berggasse 19 may have found it disconcerting when Freud left Martha and the others to make all the conversation at table.[151] Yet this clearly did not impair the overall atmosphere of the house, and visitors were full of praise for the pleasant and cordial company of Martha and Sigmund, possibly sensing that the two of them considered no sacrifice too great for their guests. Martha would on occasion even have a chicken prepared in honour of her visitors, a dish that was not otherwise served because of her husband's aversion to poultry: 'Let them stay alive and lay eggs', he would say.[152]

As Freud's fame increased, hordes of psychoanalysts were drawn to the Berggasse or to that year's summer residence. Only a few can be mentioned here. One particularly popular figure at home, who was always welcome during their holidays as well, was Sándor Ferenczi.[153] Not only was Ferenczi one of the few people to share Freud's passion for antiquities,[154] but he was someone who bubbled over with ideas and knew how to convey this effervescence to others. With his gift for telling entertaining stories he won over the children as well. Equally popular in the Freud household, and for similar reasons, was Oskar Pfister, a Protestant pastor from Zurich. One of the reasons his visits to the Berggasse went down so well was that he did not just talk shop and never ignored either Martha or the children.[155] This sense of well-being was shared, and even after fifteen years the pastor was still enthusing about how he had fallen in love with the 'cheerful-free spirit' of the Freud family. Ernest Jones, who had turned to psychoanalysis at an early stage, likewise belonged to the intimate circles of the household, and was one of the few gentiles close to Freud. The author of what was for a long time the authoritative biography of Freud, Jones focused his rapidly developing commitment to psychoanalysis on the Anglo-Saxon world, Canada and the north-eastern United States.

As psychoanalysis went from strength to strength, the ambience in the house became more and more cosmopolitan. People from virtually all corners of the earth – among them a number of the celebrities of the time – thronged to the Berggasse, whether as patients or guests. Among the most illustrious were Queen Elisabeth of Belgium, as well as Prince Dominique Radziwill and his wife Eugénie, the daughter of Marie Bonaparte.[156] Born a Bavarian princess, Elisabeth had in 1900 married Albert of Belgium and was considered an unconventional woman with an artistic bent. She played the violin and sculpted a bust of Marie Bonaparte, who had presumably been responsible for establishing her contact with Freud.[157] It was also through Marie Bonaparte that Princess Eugénie came to belong to the circle of people who spent the summers together with the Freuds, as in 1929 at the Bavarian resort of Berchtesgaden.[158] Eugénie, however, kept a greater distance from psychoanalysis than her mother did.

More and more people unrelated to medicine – including the intellectual avant-garde and artists of all orientations – came to count themselves, in spirit at least, as followers of the great psychoanalyst, and considered it to their advantage to associate with him. Albert Einstein and Gustav Mahler crossed Freud's path; letters were exchanged with many others; and in her house Martha personally met a number of the intellectual giants of the time, including Rainer Maria Rilke.[159] A particularly welcome guest was Thomas Mann, who visited the Freuds for the first time in March 1932. The writer and the professor proved to be kindred spirits, each of them – in their own different way – torn between the bourgeois and the bohemian. Yet Martha too laid claim to the Nobel prize-winner's time, and monopolized their guest. Like her sister, she was an avid reader of Mann,[160] and felt closely bonded to her 'semi fellow-countryman',[161] with whom she talked, among other things, of the Hanseatic roots they had in common.

The close friends of the Freud household also included women as famous as Lou Andreas-Salomé, Princess Marie Bonaparte and Yvette Guilbert. Lou Andreas-Salomé (1861–1937) was an impressive personality who had first joined Freud's circle at the age of fifty in 1911, when she took part in the Weimar Congress of Psychoanalysts. Born in Russia into a prosperous and cultured family, she had made a name for herself as an author and published novellas, poems and essays. Brilliant of intellect and nonconformist in lifestyle, she counted many writers among her friends. She had been the last and deepest love of Friedrich Nietzsche and for a while also Rilke's lover and muse. She was married to the Göttingen professor of orientalism, Friedrich Carl Andreas, yet this was more or less only on paper: their arrangement excluded sexual relations. Though attached to her husband, she went her own way through life, while with her knowledge and consent – indeed at her express request – her husband found consolation with the couple's housemaid. She later made his daughter from this liaison her heiress.[162] Lou Andreas-Salomé was attracted to talented and intelligent men, and fell in love time after time. In many people's eyes a charismatic femme fatale, she regarded herself as an independent, freethinking woman and her affairs as stages on an individual path of personal and artistic development.[163]

Her encounter with psychoanalysis and its famed circles was of enormous consequence for her. She was soon one of the close friends of the family and a great admirer of Martha Freud, as Martha was of her. She was impressed in particular by the mutual esteem in which Sigmund and Martha held one another, as well as by Martha's calm self-assurance.[164] In his letters to Lou Andreas-Salomé, Freud referred jokingly – but tellingly – to their shared 'Daughter-Anna', as it were replacing Martha with Lou, who was exactly the same age. Freud had in fact hit the nail on the head: for Anna, Lou had proved a source of loving care and a vital model for emulation.[165] They would meet and talk, Lou stretched out on the divan meditating aloud, Anna at her feet listening intently – a set up that was misapprehended by some as a form of alternative analysis.[166] The older woman embodied for the younger one a kind of synthesis of ideals: on the one hand, Lou was a very attractive, feminine woman, much desired by men, a gentle poet and philosophizing artist; she was beautiful, with her soft contours and thick, wavy hair. This model of femininity came close to the type of woman favoured by Martha, and perhaps secretly – more than she suspected – Anna would have liked to be a little like this herself. On the other hand, Lou was a trained psychoanalyst who knew how to observe people with 'masculine' accuracy, capable of making sharp analyses and producing daring formulations. She was also independent, sophisticated and unconventional, and took the sort of liberties normally only granted to men. To this extent she belonged to the world of Sigmund Freud, a world to which Anna was also drawn.[167] Yet for all the admiration she felt, Anna was unable simply to follow Lou's example: while Lou allowed herself to do whatever she wanted, Anna had 'surrendered' her 'impulses'[168] and lived a life that was in the broadest sense ascetic.

Along with Lou Andreas-Salomé, who in 1913 returned to Göttingen and practised there as an analyst until old age, another of the most important associates of the Freuds in the 1920s was the French Princess Marie Bonaparte (1882–1962). Marie had been quick to establish herself as an intimate friend of the family, and spared no personal effort when it came to helping and supporting Freud. Their fondness for one another was not merely a product of their resemblance in terms of courage or devotion to scientific goals, and although the fascination of rank and wealth also formed part of Marie's charms, it was not as a fairy princess that Freud valued her. Rather, it was because she was 'not an aristocrat at all, but a real person'.[169] In spite of her in many respects privileged status, she had hitherto led a life that was anything but fulfilling or satisfying.

Marie was a great-granddaughter of Napoleon I's brother Lucien Bonaparte, and was married to Prince George of Greece, the younger brother of King Constantine I.[170] Through him she belonged to the royal families of Denmark, Russia and England. Marie's ancestors had made a habit of getting involved in romantic attachments unbefitting their station and frequently in contradiction with their dynastic interests. From her mother, who had died as a result of an embolism just a few weeks after giving birth, Marie had inherited a great fortune accumulated by what were rumoured to be not always entirely honest means, including railway and casino businesses in Monte Carlo.[171] Yet the glamour and affluence had its downside. Marie had to endure frequent separations and grew up in considerable isolation in an atmosphere of emotional austerity, looked after mainly by the domestic staff and by her strict paternal grandmother, Princesse Pierre. As a girl, she felt lonely and guilty on account of her mother's death, and was prone to despondency and introspection. Her father, Prince Roland Bonaparte, an ambitious and distinguished geographer, had neither time nor interest in paying much attention to his young daughter. Marie took refuge in the world of words, and between the ages of seven and ten recorded her thoughts in notebooks in the form of stories. For a long time she forgot all about them, until many years later she came across them again as she was looking through her father's estate. Rereading them confirmed her sense of subjection to vague anxieties. Her arranged marriage to Prince George, who was substantially older than she was, produced two children, Eugénie and Pierre, and provided her with security, status and a relationship of respectful friendship, but neither true happiness nor the intimacy she yearned for. After a while, she tried to find this fulfilment outside their marriage. One of her lovers was the French statesman Aristide Briand. Meanwhile, her husband Prince George, latently homosexual, grew very close to his uncle, Prince Waldemar of Denmark, ten years his senior. For her part, Marie felt ill at ease with her role as a woman. There was something about a woman's existence that she found humiliating, and she yearned for a male identity. Within this context, she experienced Freud's writings as a key to her own psychological conflicts. For the princess, psychoanalysis was in a sense the beginning of her 'real life',[172] while for Freud the princess was a 'historic' analysand.[173]

She wrote several letters asking the professor to receive her, and offered to be his disciple. Freud was initially sceptical, suspecting that she might be just a jaundiced dilettante from high society. Single-minded as she was, however, Marie would not take no for an answer and went to see him in person. The tall forty-three-year-old – beguiling in appearance, her exquisitely feminine wardrobe coupled with a hint of aristocratic severity – made an unexpectedly deep impression on Freud, who judged her to be a courageous, extremely intelligent woman of great integrity. She told him that she had wanted to be a doctor, but that her father, whose first concern was a marriage befitting her station, had not allowed this. She had turned to medicine on her own account and worked in the psychiatric clinic of Sainte-Anne, winning the confidence of many of the female patients. She had listened in astonishment as they told her of their sexual disorders. Many claimed they were frigid, a problem with which the Princess herself was not unacquainted. Under a pseudonym, she had published an article, 'Considerations on the Anatomical Causes of Frigidity in Women', pointing out that many women only obtained satisfaction from a clitoral orgasm. Activities of this sort, especially in a woman from an aristocratic background, were anything but usual. Having heard about Freud, Marie Bonaparte decided to realize her old dream and devote herself to serious medical research. Her intention was to focus on the study of female sexuality, and to this end she wanted to begin a training analysis that would start by working through the content of her childhood notebooks. And so it came about. She talked with Martha about aspects of sexuality in Freud's work,[174] and continued to disregard conventions and etiquette, her life henceforth a balancing-act between receptions at court and sessions at Freud's. This cooperation was the start of a wonderful friendship between the princess and the professor. Freud found in Marie Bonaparte a tireless benefactress and a generous helper. For her, knowing Freud was the 'greatest happiness' of her life.[175]

A further exceptional woman who formed part of the Freud family circle was Yvette Guilbert (1865–1944). The French *diseuse* and singer had first come to the public attention with her mesmerizing appearances in Paris cafés, and soon acquired international fame. She was also immortalized through the work of Henri de Toulouse-Lautrec,[176] who painted her on several occasions wearing her trademark long black gloves. Freud had an original lithograph among his picture collection. He had first heard the audacious singing voice of Madame Guilbert in 1889, when he was in Paris for the International Congress for Experimental and Therapeutic Hypnotism. As chance would have it, in the 1920s he met her personally: Anna had become friends with Eva Rosenfeld, the niece of Yvette's husband Max Schiller. In 1929 and 1930, when Freud was suffering from cancer, Yvette's much-acclaimed concerts in Vienna were the only distraction that could entice him out of the house,[177] his appearance there causing a certain stir and not a few murmurings.[178] After all, for the sensibilities of the time, Yvette's notorious performances were no less transgressive than Freud's contentious theories. In a strange way, the professor and the *chanteuse* were perhaps kindred spirits, both of them holding up a mirror to humanity at large. Freud paid virtually no attention to the excited whisperings that followed his visits to her concerts, and seemed indifferent to the gossip all around him. Certain customs came to accompany Guilbert's annual guest appearances in Vienna: Freud would traditionally send her flowers, while in November 1931 Martha sent her a 'Russian' present. In her note of thanks, the celebrated *chanteuse* would invite Sigmund and Martha, as well as Anna, for tea in her luxury suite at the Hotel Bristol.[179]

Dorothy Tiffany Burlingham (1891–1979), another woman from the Freud circle, was not just a friend but one of the family. The daughter of the wealthy New York painter and glass artist Louis Comfort Tiffany, heir to the legendary New York jewellery company,[180] Dorothy had in 1914 married the surgeon Robert Burlingham, with whom she had four children. After separating from her manic-depressive husband, in 1925 she moved to Vienna with the children, hoping to find new orientation and above all have her eldest son Bob treated for his asthma – and have treatment herself.[181] Bob was analysed by Anna Freud, and before long the two women were intimate friends and neighbours. A special, symbiotic sort of house-sharing arrangement developed, with their two flats – one above the other at Berggasse 19 – even connected by an internal telephone.[182] Anna and Dorothy were inseparable, though Anna was always keen to deny the persistent rumour that she was a lesbian. In the 1930s, they spent many weekends together at their idyllic farm cottage Hochrotherd near Vienna. They would head here as often as possible in Dorothy's car, and it was here also that Martha's seventy-first birthday celebrations were held.[183] Martha was on particularly good terms with Dorothy, often better than with Anna. Though at times irritated that her daughter was still unmarried, she considered it fortunate that Dorothy was there, and it was with and through Dorothy that

Anna for her part was able to compensate for her 'troubled relations' with Martha.[184] In London, Anna and Dorothy later created their lifework, starting by looking after war orphans. Even though the setting might change, their creative comradeship in life and work was to last half a century.

One of Martha's most unusual friends was Bertha Pappenheim (1859–1936), who achieved fame as a champion of women's rights. The daughter of one of the legal guardians from Martha's childhood, Bertha Pappenheim was born into a wealthy Jewish family from the Viennese upper classes. She was on friendly terms with Martha especially in the 1880s and 1890s, paying her visits and also appearing in her correspondence of the time.[185] Under the name of Anna O., she became the first ever patient in the annals of psychoanalysis.

In December 1880, the doctor Josef Breuer, Freud's mentor and close friend,[186] had been called to attend her. Breuer was famed for his 'golden hand', and many of his patients came from medical circles. His renown was based on his diagnostic skill: he was said to have something akin to a sixth sense for the hidden causes of an illness. In Bertha Pappenheim, Breuer was confronted with a highly intelligent young woman now confined to her bed. For years previously she had devoted herself exclusively to the monotonous run of domestic chores, for her parents had forbidden her any further education once she finished girls' high school. Bertha had escaped into a world of strange daydreams, her 'private theatre' as she called it, in which she lived out her fantasies. When her father fell seriously ill in July 1880, she undertook to look after him, yet her own health suffered as well. The first symptoms were bouts of weakness, loss of appetite and anaemia. In the course of examining her Breuer discovered – largely by chance – a strange disorder that over the following period would worry him more than the cough he had been called in to cure. The young woman frequently lapsed into an absent-minded, trance-like condition. In addition, she suffered from obsessions: she experienced frightening hallucinations in her room, underwent rapid swings of mood, complained about darkness inside her head, and was worried about going blind and deaf. At times she had severe headaches, while at others she suffered from paralyses in one side of her face, or in an arm or leg. Her speech became incoherent: she forgot words, grew confused in her syntax and grammar, and on occasions lost the power of speech altogether. There were times during her illness when she seemed to have been pushed into a second frame of consciousness where she became a completely different person.

After a year of illness, her father died. Bertha Pappenheim fell into a state of deep melancholy, no longer recognized anyone, and would hardly eat. For all his efforts, Dr Breuer, one of the most distinguished authorities in his field, could not find a cause for her hysteria, yet Bertha had gone into a steady decline and was threatening to die in his care. There seemed to be nothing he could do to help her. But then fate came to his aid. He realized that Bertha was not living in June or July 1881; in her imagination it was still 1880, the time when she had been nursing her father. It was clear – and Breuer found further corroboration in her diaries – that Bertha had as it were hypnotized herself and was taking refuge in a memory. Yet if she could hypnotize herself, he felt, then *he* could hypnotize her too – and in the process show her the way back to health. It worked. Breuer succeeded in suggesting to her that she was capable of eating after all. He reassured her that her sight and hearing were intact, and convinced her that her paralyses would disappear as soon as she wanted them to. He also impressed upon her that – even though her father had died – she would be able to continue a normal life free from melancholy and without crying out in pain after just a few hours' sleep. Breuer went through all her symptoms, eliminating them one by one. After a while Bertha was capable of expressing what was tormenting her without prior hypnosis. She spoke freely, soon returning to her native German from the English she had often been using before. She referred to this procedure (in English) as her 'talking cure', and it did her good. Despite certain setbacks, after eighteen months of treatment Breuer was very satisfied with the results. Yet in the course of the treatment there occurred one grotesque episode he would have preferred to forget – one that sheds a different light on the course of events. On one of his visits, he found his young patient lying in bed, doubled up with pain, gasping that the child of his she was expecting was about to come! Horror-stricken, Breuer took flight and broke off the treatment in June 1882.

This classic case is one of the best known from the early days of psychoanalysis. Bertha is interpreted as having been incapable of open protest.[187] Her father's grave illness had clearly caused her much distress, and she was reproaching herself severely for not having been the perfect nurse. Breuer managed to gain access to her hidden emotions, and with time she was able to dispense with the protection provided by her symptomatology. In the process, however, her feelings for her doctor became deeper, encompassing gratitude and affection – indeed, she had probably fallen in love with him, something that he himself failed, or refused, to see. Breuer was feeling increasingly ill at ease with the case, and the situation gathered a momentum of its own. When Bertha then fantasized that she was expecting his child, he gave the treatment up, although in his *Studies on Hysteria*, co-published with Freud in 1895, he conveyed the impression that by then she was better, indeed back to normal. In fact, he had referred her to Robert Binswanger's sanatorium Bellevue at Kreuzlingen in Switzerland, where she spent almost half a year. Further periods in sanatoriums were to follow, before she moved to Frankfurt with her mother in 1888.

It was here that Bertha Pappenheim began something akin to a new lease of life. In the course of the 1890s, the famous Anna O. developed into a pioneering champion of (Jewish) women's rights. She looked after single pregnant women and committed herself to the battle against prostitution. Having once vented her own more or less covert sexual desires through the symptoms of her illness, Bertha now came to the aid of unmarried and abandoned women, while her own life grew increasingly solitary and ascetic. In this way, she placed herself above the girls who had done what she had never allowed herself to do, helping those who gave expression to their sexuality but were made outcasts for doing so. Henceforth she fought for her work and her moral and religious convictions. She remained detached from psychoanalysis for the rest of her life.[188]

In his bewilderment, Breuer had repeatedly consulted Freud about this remarkable case, and Freud had in turn kept his sweetheart up to date,[189] so Martha was perfectly well informed even when her fiancé dropped only the most veiled of hints. For her it was clear that only something unspeakable could have prompted Breuer to break off the treatment so abruptly, and she realized that it must have been something of a sexual nature.[190] Later in life Martha continued to follow her friend's fortunes. W. Ernest Freud has recalled how she and Minna would sit together, bent over their knitting, the two of them in 'absolute silence, which was then suddenly interrupted by just two words'. His grandmother would utter Bertha's name. 'Then nothing, just more silence, and Aunt Minna would nod.'[191]

Martha as a Mother

There is a Jewish proverb that says: 'God could not be everywhere at once, and so he created mothers.' The deep love characteristic of the typical Jewish mother, as well as her self-centred, overbearing, hypercritical personality – together with the ambivalence inherent in the bond to such a preterhuman being – have been the subject of stories, film comedies and caricatures. Every bit a Jewish mother, Martha Freud made her life revolve around this role, yet she did so without conforming to the cliché of the possessive Mama who stifles her children with too much love.

After a year of marriage Sigmund and Martha Freud, radiant with happiness, announced the birth of their baby daughter Mathilde. As she was the first child to be born in the *Sühnhaus*, the emperor sent a messenger with a special congratulatory letter. Five more children followed in the next eight years, three sons and two more daughters. The girls were named after friends' wives, such as Mathilde Breuer, who during her first pregnancy had supported Martha in both word and deed. The boys were given the names of people Freud admired, such as Jean Martin Charcot. The rapid succession of pregnancies took a great physical toll on the delicate young mother, in particular the last one: 'Martha is really quite miserable', wrote Freud. 'I wish it were over.'[192]

Martha had her first baby on a Sunday, the day her husband was most likely to be free from his duties. She had gone into labour the night before, but after examining her the obstetrician Dr Lott declared as expected that it could take hours. Events were to bear him out in this. Martha was initially calm and collected, yet even when the contractions increased and she could no longer stifle her screams of pain, she is said – in keeping with her characteristic self-control – to have apologized each time she shouted. Indeed, in the midst of her pain Martha was still joking with those around her, to the amusement of the doctor and midwife and the additional consternation of the father-to-be. After a difficult delivery – Mathilde had to be delivered using forceps – and the welcome news that the newborn baby was healthy and unharmed, Martha had a sense of infinite relief, and before long was feeling perfectly well. She had a spontaneous craving for a plate of soup, after which she fell asleep exhausted. Her behaviour had made an immense impression on her husband, opening up to him a new side of her personality. Although he had always 'treasured the priceless possession [he had] acquired in her', he wrote, he had never 'seen her so magnificent in her simplicity and goodness as on this critical occasion, which after all doesn't permit any pretences'.[193]

Martha did not breastfeed all her babies. Anna was bottle-fed with Gärtner's whole milk for babies, newly on the market.[194] Martin, the eldest of the boys, had not been given his mother's milk either. As was quite common for the time,[195] they fell back on the services of a wet nurse. It remains uncertain whether medical or practical factors were decisive here or whether it was a refusal on Martha's part, recoiling or silently protesting at yet another burden, especially in the case of Anna.[196]

The children of Martha and Sigmund Freud were, in the best sense of the word, well brought up: they were 'well behaved, not cowed'.[197] As Freud wrote to Wilhelm Fliess in 1896, 'Martha is well and cheerful; the rascals are splendid.'[198] In her attitudes to bringing up children, Martha was a typical representative of her generation and social background. Middle-class Jewish women like Martha were renowned for being particularly diligent custodians of German culture, teaching their children faultless manners, refinement and conduct that befitted their sex, and urging them to be responsible, reliable and trustworthy. Character formation and the inculcation of ethical values were the pillars of a good education,[199] which Martha too regarded as fundamental. She raised the children with a firm and yet kind hand, set great store by justice, and encouraged them to share even the smallest of things.[200] She had a legendary aversion to ill-discipline and sloppy dressing – no sailor suit went unironed, no dress unstarched, no shoe unpolished – and she was equally unrelenting when it came to unpunctuality or a lack of due formality. She attached great importance to good manners, and not only at mealtimes. Yet when the family later acquired a dog, this domestic etiquette was blatantly infringed – albeit by her own husband. Although it had riled her from the outset, Martha was unable to prevent Sigmund feeding the dog scraps of food at table. She did not approve of such generosity during the meal – indeed she found it positively infuriating – but there was nothing she could do about it, especially as Anna was just as inclined to spoil the animal: father and daughter alike treated the dog 'like a child'.[201] Martha's strict attitude towards feeding dogs did not mean she was not fond of the animals. Anna Freud later described the affection they had felt for their chow Lun and their genuine grief when it was run over and killed in 1929.[202] For Martha, it was simply a matter of discipline.

In many respects Martha was uncompromising, yet in others she was more broad-minded than her mother, for example, had been. As a wife she broke away from the strict religious orthodoxy that had been decisive in her own upbringing, and she raised her children in a more open and liberal spirit. She was not one to indulge in recriminations or make mountains out of molehills. Even the odd more dramatic episode was handled without much fuss, as exemplified by an incident that took place during a family holiday at Riva on Lake Garda. Once, during a sailing expedition that her children had rather recklessly embarked upon, Martha found herself looking on from the bank as their adventure threatened to turn into disaster. All of a sudden the wind had freshened, and – no matter what the young seamen might try with the tiller and mainsheet – the boat had stopped obeying their instructions. As it pitched and tossed among the stormy waves and the dancing white horses, the mast swinging dangerously from side to side, they were rapidly carried off course. Yet Martha, who was neither a swimmer nor a sailor, dashed to the nearest boat for hire moored at the pier and set out to save her children as they struggled for dear life against the wind and the current. And save them she did. Under full sail Mama's lifeboat made straight for the children's half-submerged vessel and escorted them back to the safety of the tiny, rocky port. Back on terra firma once again, Martha proceeded as if nothing had happened. There was no sermon.[203] This was typical of Martha: her manner was to keep her composure, do the right thing, keep things in perspective, and be lenient where possible.

For all their tolerance in such matters, parental authority and knowing where the limits lay were inviolate pedagogical principles in the Freud household. When it came to practical questions of upbringing it was Martha who was boss. According to Martin Freud, his mother insisted that their father should never have to do the work of a nanny: changing the nappies will not have been a task he was familiar with. Further, he was barred from undertaking field studies around the home. Psychoanalytic ideas had no business in the children's room: Martha would never have countenanced experiments of this sort.[204] Her children were not to be scientific objects. There was a more or less tacit understanding: this far, but no further.

Martha set strict limits to what was allowed, therefore, which could sometimes lead to undue inflexibility in her treatment of the children. Like many late Victorian mothers, she set great store by bodily cleanliness and hygiene and the suppression of drives,[205] sometimes at the expense of sympathy and understanding. Once, when one of the children had a high temperature and the governess suggested calling a doctor, Martha is said to have barked: 'How can I telephone the doctor? I don't yet know myself what the matter with the child is.' Her daughter Anna at least seems rarely to have succeeded in seeing the funny side of such behaviour.[206] Another incident illustrates the equanimity that Martha could at times display to the not inconsiderable irritation of those around her. When Martin – swinging upside-down from a trapeze hung in a doorway – on one occasion cracked his head open on a piece of furniture and hurt himself 'somewhat seriously' in the process, Martha simply looked up briefly from her sewing and calmly asked the governess to call a doctor, showing not the least sign of agitation, let alone panic.[207]

Within the family her husband too behaved differently from what one might have expected from a psychoanalyst.[208] Like his wife he was almost always equally kind, patient and loving, yet at the same time he was generally rather remote from the family's conflicts and daily problems. It was not usual, at least, for there to be family conferences or detailed conversations about how one was feeling, and in the private household of the great taboo-breaker sexuality was not an issue that was talked about: his sons were sent to the family doctor to learn about the facts of life.[209] However unconventional Freud may have been professionally, in his attitudes towards raising children he was guided, like his wife, by bourgeois values, laying weight on order, punctuality, good manners, moral standards and a life beyond reproach. Even when the children had grown up, he wanted to know nothing of love affairs (Martin was apparently not averse to serious flirtation) or divorces (he is said to have simply erased from his memory the failed marriage of his son Oliver).[210]

The period following the birth of their sixth child saw the emergence of a strange disorder, as Martha developed what Freud termed a *Schreiblähmung* or 'writing paralysis'.[211] After five relatively uncomplicated pregnancies something seemed to be wrong with the sixth from the outset. Martha felt unwell and listless, was paler than usual, her face was puffy, and her teeth hurt. Exhausted as she was, thirty-four-year-old Martha had already misinterpreted the first signs of the pregnancy as her menopause.[212] It was a good three months after Anna's birth, and coinciding with a visit to her mother in Hamburg and the Fliess family in Berlin, that the disorder first appeared. It denied her one of her favourite pastimes, for she found herself no longer able to produce the characteristically neat calligraphy with which she had taken such pleasure in writing her letters. It was as though she had been robbed of the power of the (written) word, and was no longer in full possession of a means of communication and a creative possibility for self-expression and self-disclosure.[213]

Was this a form of resistance, a way of withdrawing into herself, or was it self-punishment? A 'writing paralysis' characterized by manifest motor failures would bring Martha's short-term symptom complex close to a conversion neurosis, in other words the sort of disorder from the tradition of classical hysteria where a mental experience produces a somatic manifestation.[214] Unlike the psychovegetative disturbances from which Sigmund Freud himself suffered,[215] this type of psychogenic organ-function disorder is distinguished by the symbolic character of the symptom formation. In a conversion symptom, an unconscious desire that has been subject to personal censorship is represented in an encoded form, the problem thus finding symbolic expression through the disorder. A disobedient (writing) hand might thus encipher: I no longer wish or am no longer able or allowed to achieve, produce or do anything. The somatization of what cannot otherwise be expressed provides release as a compromise solution between a pressing desire and the impossibility of satisfying it.

In his treatise 'Inhibitions, Symptoms and Anxiety' (1926), Martha's husband associated motor paralyses, including the inability to make 'a liquid flow out of a tube onto a piece of white paper', with eroticization and sexuality. The fear of self-abandon and the ensuing mental blockage can be displaced indirectly onto the act of writing. The question is whether Freud's theory also applies to Martha. Perhaps she was unable to give herself over to sexual pleasure because the two of them, as Sigmund himself admitted, were afraid of further pregnancies? Or because her husband, immersed in his research work with an egocentricity that culminated in his self-analysis, was breaking new ground and in this respect himself changing? How did she view her husband's confidant of the time, the impressive Berlin ear, nose and throat specialist Wilhelm Fliess, with his lively, dark eyes, his black hair and his engaging manner? What did she make of the new scientific interests of the two men? Unable to make sense of the questions that were besetting her, taking temporary refuge in her symptoms was perhaps the natural response for Martha to make.

The Freud Family

Martin Freud wrote in his memoirs that if there existed such a thing as a happy childhood, then he and his brothers and sisters had had one.[216] The holidays always held the promise of adventure, but even everyday life at Berggasse 19 was far from monotonous or boring. Only rarely are the brothers and sisters said to have argued. For the most part they lived together in harmony, a remarkable state of affairs for such a large and complex family. The liberal atmosphere in the family was unusual for the time, and the children were very much aware of this. They were freely allowed to express their views and opinions, be inquisitive, and ask questions, and these questions were given impartial and objective answers. Their parents were appreciative when they showed themselves keen to learn or were successful at school, but they did not overemphasize such success or put pressure on them to achieve it. There was discipline and hierarchy without the need for authoritarian commands: the children were respected as persons in their own right. The rules of good conduct that were imparted did not preclude fun and exuberance. In the Freud household, psychoanalytic educational theory was put into sensible practice: it was 'modern openness reined in by middle-class decorum'.[217]

Nonetheless, this apparently smooth façade was not without its cracks and fissures. What price did the family pay for their harmony? Many things in the Freud household were presumably swept under the carpet, for Freud's domination within the family, in conjunction with his and Martha's inhibitions, it has been argued, engendered 'a network of expectations, demands and assumptions that were not spoken about'.[218] Many an issue will have thus gone by the board, and the inventor of the talking cure – 'chimney sweeping', as Bertha Pappenheim had called it – and his family themselves probably resorted more to non-verbal communication. Perhaps the professor found it easier to talk about other people's problems than his own. In such an atmosphere of taciturnity, the members of the Freud family may often have found it difficult to maintain, cultivate and develop their own inner world, since by doing so they ran the risk of infringing some more or less unspoken law. Accordingly they strove to read between the lines, with the corresponding danger of mistakes and misdemeanours. On the other hand, outbursts of aggression were frowned upon, as comes to light in the account given by one of the grandchildren, W. Ernest Freud,[219] which tells of no such incidents within the family. Self-control was sacrosanct.

However it may have come about, this was the peaceable and loving community – with its extended-family structure so fundamentally different from the typical nuclear family of today – in which the children grew up. Proud as he was of what he fondly called his 'rabble', Freud gave the impression of being a kindly, well-nigh perfect paterfamilias, and Martha was regarded as a conscientious mother. The two of them only ever had the children's best interests in mind, and were keen to ensure that as far as possible they should be wanting for nothing. It was a matter of great importance, in their eyes, that the children should always be well dressed, something they considered vital for their bearing and self-esteem. Freud did not want them to endure the privations he had undergone in his childhood and youth: he provided them with pocket money as was appropriate and was always as generous as the general circumstances allowed. As their demands became greater with the passing of the years, he put the royalties from his books to one side for his children.[220] These dividends came without any subliminal strings attached, moreover, for, as Martha herself made clear, her husband had no interest in the children following in his footsteps, indeed he preferred them not to.[221] The parents left their children to their own devices in such matters, although as middle-class intellectuals they naturally fostered their cultural interests, encouraged them to read books, and took them to museums and galleries. If the daughters went to the theatre, Freud would time his habitual evening stroll so that he could pick them up and accompany them home, listening attentively to their accounts of what they had seen. He taught the children to play tarock, and often found the odd moment to play a round with them. The special hobby that Martha passed on to her daughters was her ornate needlework. Almost all the women in the family were experts in crocheting, while Anna later switched to weaving and knitting. Throughout her life Anna made all her own clothes by hand,[222] a passion that prompted her father to comment: 'If the day comes when there is no more psychoanalysis, you can be a seamstress in Tel Aviv.'[223]

As Mathilde, Martin and Oliver were born while the Freuds still lived in the *Sühnhaus*, whereas the younger three arrived after the move to the Berggasse, the six Freud children were naturally divided into two threesomes. The older trio were looked after first by a shared nursemaid and then during their first school years by a shared governess. Like their younger siblings, they had one passion in common: all the Freud children were stout royalists, and took delight in everything they heard or saw that came from the Imperial Court. The very sight of the magnificent *Hofwagen*, or Coach of the Court, with its liveried coachman, was enough to hold them spellbound.[224] This was perhaps the mother's influence: Martha was a patriotic follower of the German imperial family and was to a certain degree guided by its lifestyle, dressing and grooming the boys after the fashion of the young princes.[225] The brothers Martin and Ernst became special companions, going sailing, ice-skating and hiking together, while Oliver was more of a loner. He was not interested in sport, and preferred to pursue interests such as mathematics and drawing. Martin and later on in particular Ernst assumed the role of big brothers, while Oliver enjoyed the protection of his older sister Mathilde, to whom he was very attached. Mathilde and Sophie were united by their shared predilection for all things beautiful and their passion for 'the understated elegance their mother cultivated'.[226] Even though Anna was just as girlish in appearance as her two elder sisters, Mathilde and Sophie came over as more 'feminine', yet it was Annerl – as the baby of the family – who was given special protection by Martin, who taught her to swim and took her hiking with him.

The relationships within the sextet were complex and convoluted, which was especially significant because there were times when the children only had limited contact with other children of the same age from outside the family: in an attempt to avoid infections and protect their offspring against serious disease, the parents for a while hired a governess to come to the flat to teach them.[227] Even so, this did not keep other children away, and on one occasion Freud wrote of a 'children's party, twenty individuals strong' to celebrate Mathilde's birthday.[228] They tended to mix predominantly with children from nearby Jewish middle-class families, but this changed when it came to going to school on a daily basis. The family was thus particularly eager to hear the accounts given by Martin, the first of the children to be sent to school, when he attended the final year of primary school: brothers, sisters and parents alike were a rapt audience as he told of his experiences. Although being taught at home in isolation was hardly ideal preparation, at least in social terms,[229] all the Freud children were good pupils and got accordingly good marks at school. Oliver and Anna did particularly well, while Martin's achievements at times left a little to be desired, as his mother was dismayed to learn at the parents' days that were regularly held.[230] One factor that played a part in the matter of scholarly success or failure was that all the children except Mathilde were hampered by a serious lisp, which, as Anna Freud later pointed out, severely impaired their school performance. Their speech impediment was apparently so acute that the teachers complained that something had to be done about it. Measures were taken: a speech therapist was hired, and the lisping stopped.

Once the children had grown up, their parents were beset by new worries. The First World War was a particularly bad time. A wave of patriotism had taken hold of Vienna and the whole country, and as the situation grew more critical the events did not fail to leave their mark on Martha. In her consternation she clutched at any straw for comfort: on the back of a piece of paper with a recipe on it she even jotted down some astrological 'prophecies for the World War'.

Martin Freud volunteered, as did Ernst later on, while Oliver served as an engineer constructing tunnels. Sigmund and Martha thus had to look on as all three sons went off to war. Sigmund, who was going on for sixty, was too old to be called up. Although not particularly interested in politics, at the outset he too shared the fervour with which Austria made its stand and faced up to its adversaries. It was generally assumed that the army would soon put an end to the disturbances in the Balkans and rapidly re-establish order. They were worried about Anna, who was in England when war broke out, but with the aid of the Austrian ambassador she returned to Vienna safe and well. Yet day-to-day normality was slower to return. The war was disastrous for Freud's practice: patients stayed away, and income fell sharply. Martha economized, yet their circumstances became tighter and tighter. It gradually emerged that the hostilities would not be over as quickly as had been hoped. The bloodshed exceeded all expectations. Martin wrote a letter home saying that a bullet had blasted a hole in his cap and sleeve, and reports from the front told of mounting casualties.

Family photograph, 1909
From left to right: Oliver, Sophie, Minna Bernays, Martha Freud,
Mathilde, Anna, Martin, Ernst

Sigmund and Martha Freud lived in fear for their sons' lives, often going for long stretches without hearing from them. The constant dread that the war might cost them their lives or reduce them to permanent invalids almost drove them to distraction. Yet there was nothing they could do.

Vienna was now clearly suffering great poverty and hardship. Even those who still had money could buy precious little with it. Day after day Martha struggled to get hold of the absolute necessities. Meat had disappeared long ago, but with a bit of luck it was possible to find vegetables. Friends and relatives abroad sent food parcels with coffee, tea, margarine and corned beef, while Martha did her best to obtain tinned milk, porridge oats, meat extract and herbs and spices.[231] Despite the shipments of food, Sigmund, Martha, Minna and Anna lost both weight and strength. The winters were severe, and it was virtually impossible to get coal for heating. It was not infrequent for the family at Berggasse 19 to sit muffled up in thick woollen blankets in their cold, damp rooms – having sealed the cracks and gaps in the draughty, frosty windows as best they could. Their fingers numb with the cold, they would battle on with whatever they were doing, whether needlework or writing. And still there was no end to the bad news. Sophie's husband Max had been wounded, and they were constantly afraid that something might happen to their sons too. The anxiety of day-to-day existence could hardly have been greater.

When the war ended in November 1918 and the monarchy collapsed, galloping inflation soon reduced any remaining savings to worthlessness. Virtually everyone was debilitated by hunger, exhaustion, cold and disease. There was scarcely any work to be had, and even the Freud sons were unable to find any. Sigmund was struggling to provide not only for his own large family but also for his mother and sisters, supporting more than a dozen people with a practice that was as good as non-existent at the time. Not for the first time the question came up whether it might not be better to leave the bleakness of Vienna and make a new start elsewhere.[232] Yet this remained no more than an idea. The Freuds did not leave Vienna – not yet anyway. Though the situation was anything but rosy, they forced themselves to struggle on. Currency depreciation, food shortages, illness and death – for years after the war had ended the family would still have tough trials to face.

It was also in the post-war years that the children left their parental nest for good, some of them moving away from Vienna too. A number of them laid the foundations for remarkable achievements to come even in the third and fourth generations, yet not all the Freud children were equally successful in emerging from the overpowering shadow cast by the father: as Martin put it, 'no one denied that my father was a genius'.[233] The six of them developed in very different ways. Yet the family tradition of analysis has been continued through to the present.

Martha's Children

The life of the eldest daughter Mathilde (1887–1978) was over-shadowed by illness. As a six-year-old she almost died of diphtheria. In 1906, when she needed an operation for appendicitis,

Freud's old friend Ignaz Rosanes wanted to try out a new method for the ligature of blood vessels, but his experiment went wrong: a few hours after the operation Mathilde almost died from a post-operative haemorrhage. Two years later, there was further call for concern when Mathilde went down with a high temperature that seemed to suggest a dangerous peritonitis. She was sent away to a spa to recuperate, since Martha at the time also had to look after her ailing mother. Another two years on, she had to undergo a further serious operation.[234] Mathilde grew up to be a good-natured, caring and understanding sister and later on a considerable help to her mother in running the household. As Anton W. Freud remembers, she was a typical first-born child: bossy and hard to please, and in this respect not unlike her grandmother Amalie.[235] Her brother Martin regarded her as a model of good sense and kindness, and in his memoirs always spoke affectionately of the sister who several times had protected him from humiliations – something that meant a great deal to him. Within the configuration of mother and daughters, Mathilde is said to have often intervened to restore the peace and settle differences, always willing to offer advice, support and guidance. Anna's love for her eldest sister was less mixed with jealousy than her feelings for Sophie. Mathilde took keen pleasure in handicrafts, handmade fabrics and classically elegant fashion, a passion she shared with her mother that was to play an important part later in her life.

In 1909 Mathilde married the Viennese textile merchant and silk importer Robert Hollitscher (1875–1959), an at times rather misanthropic and pessimistic character whom she had met the year before in Merano.[236] The two of them lived near the Berggasse, and Mathilde continued to visit her parents frequently, usually having lunch with them. As a consequence of her operations and the ensuing complications, Mathilde remained childless.[237] She and her husband wanted to raise one of Sophie's orphaned sons, Heinerle, but in 1923 the boy died of miliary tuberculosis at the age of five. Following her emigration she proved to be a skilled business-woman, working as a fashion designer and boutique owner. Despite her delicate health, Mathilde lived to be ninety years old, dying in 1978 in London.

The second-born was Jean Martin Freud (1889–1967). The birth of a son meant a lot to the parents, and they named him after his father's great teacher, Jean Martin Charcot. For the younger children Martin was the protective big brother from whom one could learn. He worked first as a banking lawyer. Later on, he devoted himself to the affairs of the analytic publishing house, the *Verlag*, and in 1931 took over as its manager. A vital, sporting character, he remained particularly close to his parents, whom he visited every day, partly because of the tensions in his less than happy marriage to Ernestine Drucker (1896–1980), a speech therapist. Martin had married Esti on his thirtieth birthday in 1919, and had two children with her. Born in 1922, Anton Walter grew up in Vienna and after the *Anschluss* in 1938 emigrated with his father and his father's family to England – without Esti. Sophie, who was born in 1924, stayed with her mother. The two of them went first to Paris, where Esti's sister lived,[238] and Sophie later headed for the United States, where she eventually became a professor in social work and psychology in Boston. The estrangement between Martin and his wife had begun as early as 1922.[239] Sophie spoke of 'quarrels, tears and violent hysterical scenes'.[240]

Freud did not like the irascible Esti.[241] From a letter to his nephew Sam[242] it emerges that he possibly regarded her as not entirely compos mentis, or at least highly neurotic. Martha, on the other hand, is said to have got on well with her. Yet Martha had her difficulties with Martin, and their relationship was a strained one. To her displeasure, her eldest son had at the time found his way into the gossip columns, the papers reporting duels, brawls, reckless sporting exploits, injuries and accidents,[243] and for a while as a young man Martin was almost seen as the black sheep of the family. 'It is true that I got into trouble more often than my brothers and sisters. However, this had an important advantage in that I was more often rescued by father', as the mischief-maker himself admitted.[244] In a letter to Carl Jung dated 17 February 1911, Freud wrote of the difficult mother–son relationship: 'he is not his mother's favourite son.' On the contrary, Freud felt, he was treated almost unjustly by her. Freud believed that the roots for this lay in her problematic past relationship with Eli: in her behaviour towards Martin, Martha compensated for 'her overindulgence towards her brother', to whom he bore a considerable resemblance, while Freud's own treatment of his son, strangely enough, was a compensation for the severity he had once shown towards Eli.[245] In other words, Freud did not rule out the possibility that Martha was venting aggressions on her son that were directed at her brother, while he himself was reluctant to criticize Martin on account of his feelings of guilt towards Eli. One thing that is certain is that Martin's sexual dissipation[246] gave rise to rumours about which Martha remained resolutely silent. As a young man he is said to have even approached or got involved with certain of his father's analysands such as Edith Jackson[247] – Martha made no comment, though she can hardly have remained unaware of it. According to Paul Roazen, once when Martin was on his way to see a performance of *Romeo and Juliet* in London, his father was unable to resist a dig at him, commenting that Martin did not need to spend any more time studying the role of Romeo, for he already was one. Martha recognized the allusion only too well.[248]

However many eyebrows his lifestyle may have raised, Martin, who was decorated for his services in the First World War, had 'a very good and pleasant life': according to his son Anton W. Freud, 'his father facilitated his development'. After emigrating to England, both Martin and Anton W. Freud were in 1940 interned as 'enemy aliens', Martin being taken to the Isle of Man, and his son shipped to Australia. After his release Anton W. Freud in turn rendered great service to the British armed forces,[249] before building up a new life for himself as a chemical engineer. For Martin himself, things were not so easy in England, where his knowledge of law could hardly be turned to account. Even at fifty he was still 'used to his father's help'. He tried his hand in various fields and ran a shop, all in all leading 'a pleasant life in a nice part of London'.[250] His memoirs are a homage to an idealized father and the carefree childhood he spent in the Freud household. He also gave an account in person to his son, who found it easy to identify with: the Freuds were simply generous people, and Martha in general 'the kindest in the family' – albeit not one to mince her words or beat about the bush if anything was not to her liking.[251] Generous as she was, she thoroughly spoilt her grandchildren, taking young Anton shopping in Neumann's department store in Kärntner Strasse and 'fitting him out like a bride with a new set of clothes'.[252]

Martin was followed by another son, Oliver (1891–1969), who was named after Cromwell. Oliver was a particularly beautiful child, 'like an Italian', in the words of his mother. As a child he is said to have been difficult and unapproachable. His compulsive cleanliness, ritualistic orderliness and indecisiveness eventually required treatment by one of his father's colleagues. A rather solitary, cerebral child, Oliver was interested in abstract, intellectual matters and passionate about numbers, machines and the inanimate world. Freud admired the boy's theoretical bent, his great knowledge and his circumspection, and saw him as his pride and 'secret hope'[253] – partly because he was also so tractable and well behaved, which made it easy to handle him. His problematic development was thus all the more worrying to Freud. He was considered his mother's favourite son, and, like Martha, Oliver was always obsessed with precision. He had a habit of ordering the things around him and could not abide excessive laxity towards rules or inaccuracy, for example, in road signs. Always at the top of his class, Oliver later used his talents to become a civil engineer and was involved, among other things, in the construction of various important tunnels aimed at improving European rail transport. The reputation he had from an early age for being the technological whiz-kid among the hordes of Freud siblings was given an amusing illustration by the answer Anna is said to have given when one of her playmates once asked her if she knew how to use the telephone: 'No, about such things we go to ask Oliver.'[254]

After a first marriage that did not last long,[255] Oliver in 1923 married the Berlin painter and teacher Henny Fuchs (1892–1971). His mother and his brother Martin made the journey to Berlin for the wedding. Freud's comment on the marriage was that the young woman would have to summon up a good deal of 'good spirits and modesty'.[256] Initially Oliver and Henny lived in the Tempelhof district of Berlin. Given the lack of work, it was a struggle to make ends meet, so Freud sent his son a monthly sum from his Goethe

Prize fund.[257] Later they moved again, this time to Paris. Here they did not fare any better, and Martha wrote: 'Now they have been sitting over half a year in Paris and not the glimmer of a prospect!'[258] After this, Nice was their destination, where Oliver was forced to give up his career as an engineer, and instead became the owner of a photographic shop.[259] From occupied France they fled to the United States, where Oliver died in 1969 in North Adams, Massachusetts. Tragic was the fate of his only child Eva (1924–44), described by Martha as a 'sweet child, of all my grandchildren the closest to my heart'.[260] After the family had already tried and failed to make a dramatic escape over the Pyrenees to Spain, Eva balked at the idea of a second attempt and stayed with friends in Nice, which was under Italian sovereignty. There she developed a brain tumour[261] and died in 1944, probably from the consequences of a miscarriage.[262]

Ernst Freud (1892–1970), the next-born son and considered the most charming and stable of the boys, was, as his nephew Anton W. Freud confirmed,[263] the sort of person whom fortune smiles upon. His parents were convinced of this too, and called Ernst their 'lucky child'. This was not just because he always found the best mushrooms in the summer: almost everything Ernst tried his hand at was a success. He grew up to be very independent, expressly seeking a profession that neither his father nor anyone else in the family knew anything about. After serving in the First World War as a teacher in the artillery school in Trieste, he studied architecture in Munich and settled in Berlin as an architect. His business was highly successful, and among other things he was given the task of designing a house for the Zionist leader Chaim Weizmann.[264] Ernst Freud was also responsible for the redesign of Schloss Tegel as a sanatorium, and after his emigration to England continued to work as an architect.

In 1920 Ernst married the Berlin-born Lucie (Lux) Brasch (1896–1989). Lucie, the Freuds' favourite daughter-in-law,[265] was 'a very rich, beautiful, clever and nice girl',[266] whom everyone found enchanting. The three grandchildren were born in Berlin and live in England: Stephen, born in 1921, became a publisher; Lucian, born in 1922, is one of the most significant contemporary painters; and Clement, born in 1924, became a writer and Member of Parliament. Lucian Freud's daughter Bella is a fashion designer, and her sister Esther a writer. The two young women have clearly shown how the fourth generation today view their forefather, recounting[267] how their father was once asked by a doctor if he was related to the great psychoanalyst. The English doctor's pronunciation of 'the great Freud' made it sound like 'the great fruit', which was in turn further corrupted to 'the grapefruit'. And that was that. Even today, within family circles their progenitor is smilingly referred to as 'the grapefruit', the towering figure of Sigmund jokingly shrunk to a palm-sized citrus.

After the third son came a second daughter, Sophie (1893–1920), who was named after one of the nieces of Samuel Hammerschlag, Freud's greatly revered religion teacher. Sophie was her mother's favourite, her sunshine, and as a child is said to have been unwilling to share her mother's attentions with her brothers and sisters.[268] When she had a high temperature during a bout of measles at the age of seven or eight, in her delirium she kept calling out for 'her' mummy: few would have suspected at the time that decades later it would be the other way round, as Martha cried out repeatedly for Sophie during her final hours.

The relationship between mother and daughter was a special one. They were very close to one another, travelled together, and went to stay at health resorts with one another. This closeness was further fostered by the fact that after her marriage Sophie went to live in Hamburg, Martha's home city. Sophie was regarded as exceptionally good-looking and feminine. One of her relatives by marriage even considered her 'the most beautiful woman he had ever seen'.[269] Like her sister Mathilde she was groomed to be a wife and mother. In 1913 she married the Hamburg photographer Max Halberstadt (1882–1940), responsible for many of the portrait photos of Freud. They had met in Hamburg, where Sophie was spending a few weeks on holiday, and their prompt engagement had presented the parents with virtually a fait accompli. Sophie and Max had a short, happy marriage, which produced two sons, before they were struck by misfortune. Shortly after the First World War had ended, thousands of people were struck

Martha Freud with her daughter Sophie, about 1912

down by an influenza epidemic, including Sophie. Having herself caught and recovered from the infection that was ravaging Europe, Martha clung to the hope that if she – the mother – had got over it, then her daughter would be young and strong enough to do likewise. She was mistaken. Sophie died in January 1920, on the fourth day of a galloping influenza. Sigmund and Martha were devastated. After the death of the sister she had both admired and envied, it was Anna in particular who came to the aid of the widower Max and their children. On a number of occasions, as in the spring of 1922, she stayed in Hamburg for several weeks helping out. Sophie's death brought Anna closer not only to her father, but also to her mother.[270]

The family was dealt another heavy blow with the death of one of Sophie and Max's two sons in 1923 – the year that Eli Bernays died too. The other son, born in 1914, was W. Ernest Freud, who was to continue the family's psychoanalytical tradition down through the decades, more than fifty years of which were spent in London. He vividly recalls his first visit to Berggasse 19 at the age of two or three, and his meeting with his grandfather: 'It was my birthday, and he called to me from the bathroom. I was told to go and see him, which I did. He was sitting in the bathtub, holding a tin drum and beating it with the drumsticks. This was his birthday present for me.'[271] In 1921 Anna considered adopting 'Ernstl' and bringing him to live in the Berggasse flat, but ended up deciding against it, deeming that living with his grandparents and great-aunt would probably not have provided the proper environment for a complicated seven-year-old boy who had just lost his mother. Martha too would have found the strain of looking after Ernstl too much. Yet Anna did end up doing a great deal to support him.

Anna Freud (1895–1982) was the last-born of the six Freud children. She was named after Anna Hammerschlag, Samuel Hammerschlag's daughter. One of Sigmund's sisters was also called Anna. This sixth child came at an awkward time. Neither Martha's physical and mental reserves nor the overstretched family finances were quite up to coping with an addition to the family. Anna was aware of this, and always described her early childhood as an unhappy one. She had a sense of being the odd one out and a burden on the others.

As has already been seen, the thirty-four-year-old Martha had misread the first signs of this unwanted pregnancy as the onset of her menopause. In other words, she unconsciously equated the child she was expecting with being deprived or dispossessed of a vital part of her identity as a woman. This may be interpreted as a source of subsequent tensions, such as Anna's tendency to push her mother to one side or relieve her of her functions. A further determinant was that she was born in the year in which her father dated his discovery of the meaning of dreams, the key to psychoanalysis. Her early childhood, that is, coincided with the period of most radical change in her father's professional development, of which Freud would later say that the sort of insights he had in this period are given to a person only once in a lifetime. More than the elder children, Anna virtually grew up with psychoanalysis and felt that she and it were twins competing for the attentions of the father. Yet as though intuiting that it was a battle she could never win outright, her defence was to take the bull by the horns and – instead of competing with her imaginary antagonist – to merge with her abstract rival, making herself 'the mother of psycho-analysis'.[272] Of all the children it was 'Annerl' – the youngest and least wanted – who was to become most important to her father. Circumstances paved the way for this development from an early stage. When Freud's practice enjoyed an upturn shortly after Anna's birth, Freud interpreted her presence as a good omen for the family.[273] Before long, Freud had come to appreciate the bright little girl especially for her *Unartigkeit* or naughtiness. To a certain extent, in other words, he allowed her to behave unconventionally, while her mother was less generous in this respect.

Anna grew up, to all intents and purposes, with three mother figures: Martha, Minna and – before starting school – the Catholic nursemaid Josefine. Her bond with her mother was thus not an exclusive one. Once, on one of their walks in a park on the Ringstrasse, Anna was playing near a bench where Martha was sitting watching over her children. When Josefine disappeared from her sight for a moment, Anna went running off in panic to look for her – even though she knew full well that her mother was near at hand. She got lost, and was only found after the whole family had anxiously scoured the entire park. Many years later, Anna Freud cited the episode as proof that it had been Josefine who had made her feel safe and secure. At the same time, her actions spoke volumes about her feelings towards her mother.[274]

Anna often felt left out, and as a result sought to attract people's attention. She was her father's daughter, and relished his affection. In her relationship with her mother, by contrast, she frequently had the feeling that Martha was not open or honest with her, and that there was a great deal she hid from her. As a twelve-year-old, for example, when Anna had to go into hospital for an appendicec-tomy, she was led to believe it was merely for an examination. Even though the deception may have been motivated by a concern for

Anna's own well-being, and her father too may have had a hand in it, a surprised and angry Anna put the blame squarely on her autocratic mother.[275] Her indignation passed in time, and the following summer the episode seemed to have been forgotten. Anna went travelling with Martha, and wrote to her every day they were parted. At the same time, however, she began to dwell on how much she would like to go travelling with her father, and was full of envy towards her brothers Ernst and Oliver when they had him all to themselves for a time in Holland in 1910.

When Anna was a young girl, Martha's disapproval of her daughter's plain and unadorned taste in clothes was a source of further differences between them. Unlike her elegant mother, Anna was little given to worrying about how she looked. Indeed, she was always rather androgynous in appearance and not the least bit interested in ladies' style, cosmetics or the latest fashion[276] – though she was always happy and proud to wear the necklaces her father had given her. Anna did not view herself as particularly feminine. She regarded her life as better – in a certain sense more sublimated – than the one led by her mother, who for her part did not share Anna's vision of femininity. It was clearly above all Sophie whom their mother considered a model to be emulated and the two elder daughters who came closer to fulfilling her ideals of womanhood.[277]

This smouldering conflict was given fresh fuel by Freud's illness. Now pushing thirty, Anna wished to be close to her father, to have a place at his side, as though this were her natural due. Gradually, she sought to take over her mother's role.[278] As Martha lamented, Anna had been such a tender, sweet child, but later she proved to have a tough side.[279] For her part, Anna resented the fact that her mother had encumbered her with looking after her father and did not herself have the strength to do what was necessary.[280] Their conflict intensified when it came to the trips to Berlin for Freud's medical treatment there. Anna ignored the fact that Martha could actually look after Sigmund perfectly well, and insisted on travelling with him herself. Almost in the same breath she interpreted her mother's withdrawal as a sign of weakness. These tensions were exacerbated when Martha's strength genuinely did start to wane.

All this took place within the very confined space of the apartment at Berggasse 19. Anna lived with her mother until her mother's death, and never married. Anton W. Freud has suggested it might not have been entirely by choice that his aunt remained single, given the decimation of a generation of young men by the First World War.[281] Of the three daughters it was Anna who received the best education, and she started work as a teacher at a *Lyceum* or high school before changing course. She had begun reading her father's works as early as 1910, and in 1918 he began to analyse her. In 1920 Anna officially accompanied her father to the International Psychoanalytic Congress held in The Hague. By her late thirties her life was totally dedicated to her father and his work: she was his secretary, nurse, disciple and associate. She laid the foundations of child psychoanalysis. Ulli Olvedi cites the psychoanalyst Alex Holder, who spent twenty years in Anna Freud's circles, as saying that Anna only ever seemed really happy and relaxed when she was dealing with children.[282] Even as an elderly woman there was something of a little girl about her, with the slides she wore to hold her hair back to the sides and her preference for plain frocks. She created her own family to the extent that she took special care of her nephew W. Ernest Freud and became a mother figure not only for the children of her special companion Dorothy Tiffany Burlingham but also many others with whom she dealt through her work. Anna's extended family without a man worked. She and Dorothy were perhaps even a little like Martha and Minna. Anna only outlived her friend by a few years, and died in London in October 1982 following a stroke.

Later Years: She was 'Normal'

Berggasse 19 remained the family's focal point long after the Freud children had grown up and founded their own families, and was never a place of silence and somnolence.[283] As the years passed, the household came increasingly under a female influence. Freud knew himself to be surrounded and reliably looked after by a handful of women. The closest circle was the trio of Martha, Minna and Anna, as well as Mathilde. With the help of Paula Fichtl and the other domestic staff, Martha organized the daily routine and was the mainstay on whom the rest depended. Minna supported her in this, while Anna took care of her father's physical well-being and contributed to the dissemination of his work. However, other woman friends and family members – some of them ardent followers of his ideas – also gathered round the great man. Within the group dynamics of this heterogeneous circle, the diverse roles and functions were very much divided up between them, each of the women having a distinct position with respect to psychoanalysis and to Freud personally. Freud meanwhile benefited from the teamwork that his followers more or less tacitly negotiated. Some were responsible predominantly for his emotional health; others were primarily after a meeting of minds; still others filled the Berggasse with an aura of sophistication.[284] Paula, the housemaid, found herself with the thankless task of bearing the brunt when others let off steam. If ever anything made her angry it was always triggered by something to do with 'the power struggles between the women', in other words Martha, Minna and the female domestic staff.[285] The potential tensions inherent in such a complex family structure are obvious.

Further friends, colleagues, associates, pioneers of psychoanalysis as well as analysands from outside the inner circle likewise had their place within this overall configuration, and helped shape the Freuds' life. Some submitted to their leader, others opposed him. Many saw themselves as champions of a modern view of humankind. There were times when the Berggasse apartment became a battleground for hammering out unconventional insights – and other times when it was perhaps more like vanity fair or a platform for self-promotion. Anton W. Freud has described[286] how caring and solicitous people were towards the professor, especially since everyone shared a constant, more or less unspoken concern for his health.[287] The most trivial platitude swelled up in importance, and nobody seemed to treat Freud like a normal human being, many of the visitors playing the part of courtiers at what was both a psychoanalytical and a private court. 'The brightest star at this court was my grandmother', said grandson Anton Walter.[288] She impressed them all with her kindness, with what W. Ernest Freud has referred to as 'real love':[289] despite being so dutiful, resolute and proud in character, she radiated goodness and benevolence. Martha held the family together, it was said. Without her, the fragile structure from which psychoanalysis grew and spread would have probably come crumbling down: 'She was indispensable for the birth of psychoanalysis.'[290]

In addition, Martha was a mediator between the often conflicting personalities and characters around her. Like many partners of outstanding men, Martha did relations work 'in the shadows'.[291] Not only did she shield her husband from private discord and domestic trivialities, but she also had a talent for pouring oil on troubled waters and soothing heated tempers. On many an occasion it was Martha who placated friends and acquaintances after her hot-blooded husband had raised their hackles,[292] not a task to be underestimated considering the impulsiveness he had displayed in his youth and his tendency to break off relationships. Within the complex set-up of the Freud family enterprise, Martha – acting entirely in her husband's interest – thus played the role of intermediary, ensuring that there was a harmonious atmosphere in which controversial positions could be transformed into objectively cogent arguments instead of having a destructive effect. The heated tone of a psychoanalytical debate could in this way be tempered by the timely appearance of Frau Freud, her very presence forcing the group to interrupt the discussion at least briefly and then possibly redirecting it towards less choppy waters. It is open to question whether this interference was welcome to the participants or rather had a counterproductive effect, yet Martha was impervious to possible objections from her husband's disciples anyway.

These disciples had varying perceptions of Martha. The French psychoanalyst René Laforgue recognized Martha, whom he met in the 1920s, as a practical woman who was wonderfully skilful in creating an atmosphere of peace and good cheer. The analyst Theodor Reik noted the lucidity that enabled her to get to the heart of a matter, and once related that her response to deep psychoanalytic insights had often been the simple observation that for women many symptoms disappear after their menopause anyway, when they calm down and become resigned.[293]

One of Freud's ex-analysands from the 1930s, Albert Hirst, said that Martha was of the same 'type' as Freud's mother.[294] Mark

Brunswick, another patient, added the attribute 'ironic' to the many qualities that were ascribed to her,[295] citing an incident he had experienced one evening spent together with them, when Paul Federn, one of Freud's followers, had attempted a rather long-winded explanation of a slip of the tongue: 'It is so interesting', Martha had mocked, 'we never hear such things.' Robert Jokl, another analysand, criticized the fact that Martha had done an extraordinary amount for her husband whereas he 'did not do much for her'.[296] What Irmarita Putnam, a student of Freud's, admired about Martha was that she had managed to keep her 'equilibrium' despite all the ups and downs in Freud's career. She found her 'the most wonderful person' and thought she seemed 'the most contented woman'.[297] In the words of Eva Rosenfeld, an associate and friend of Anna's, Martha's self-control made her a 'perfect lady'.[298]

By comparison with these quite diverse recollections from Freud's disciples, there are certain characteristics that constantly recur in accounts of Martha Freud from the later years: her talent for organization, her discipline, and her prudence. Regularity in life was the be-all and end-all, she would say.[299] Yet what some people appreciated as orderliness and discipline, others felt to be compulsive pedantry. This was the case, for example, with her alleged quirk of giving her husband's doctor a ticking-off whenever he sat on Freud's bed and creased the sheets, as well as her habit of searching the house for traces of Freud's cigar ash.[300] Ernest Jones dismissed such petty claims: 'Her personality was fully developed and well integrated: it would well deserve the psychoanalysts' highest compliment of being "normal".'[301]

As the years passed, Martha continued to regulate the Freuds' domestic life in this spirit of orderliness and circumspection. The extended family in the Berggasse was an unorthodox Jewish family with its own culture and its own values, or in the words of W. Ernest Freud 'an intellectual, solidly middle-class family with high standards of decency and honesty'.[302] They were 'nice people, warm-hearted and helpful'. Along with Sigmund and Martha, in the years around 1930 this family circle consisted of Minna, Paula Fichtl and other domestic staff, Anna and the Burlingham family, as well as the 'old aunts', Sigmund's sisters. Martha continued to

Seventieth birthday, 26 July 1931

demonstrate her capacity for accepting the inevitable, if possible providing one of her dry comments for good measure. The labours of nursing would thus prompt the laconic remark: *ein Liegender braucht einen Laufenden* ('the reposing need their runners'). A person who made pretensions to goodness but whose goodness fell rather short of the mark would elicit the humorous observation: *Der ist auch kein gebratener Engel!* ('he's no roast angel either!'). In the context of one conversation about miners, she is said to have shrugged her shoulders and remarked: 'Below ground? It's bad enough above ground!' She was also much less unworldly and puritanical than her bourgeois, ladylike manner might have led one to believe. When a conversation with her grandson Ernst turned to the Hamburg Reeperbahn, Ernst was astonished to learn that Martha had herself been taken around the red-light district and apparently even seen one of the area's infamously seedy nightclubs.[303]

Illness

Looking back on many years spent living together with his wife, Freud extolled her vigorous health. In a letter to his future son-in-law Max Halberstadt he said he was thankful for the 'children who have turned out so well, and for the fact that she has neither been very abnormal nor very often ill'.[304]

In her youth, her pallor had elicited many a medical recommendation from her worried sweetheart – though in the same breath he would warn her not to let herself be 'excessively coddled'.[305] The slightest indisposition in Martha worried him. When he heard that she was unwell in the summer of 1885, he was beside himself. An autumn chill was enough for him to threaten her jokingly that if she did not get better soon he would go straight to Paris as a punishment instead of stopping off to see her in Wandsbek beforehand. He confessed that there were times when he was seized by an intense fear that she might fall ill.[306] Just why he was so vulnerable to these alarming fantasies about his wife must remain open to question. In June 1886, he suddenly started worrying about her health for no special reason, and sent her a sum of money with strict orders that it was only to be used for a holiday spent convalescing: after all, he wrote, he wanted to marry a woman who was healthy: 'If I find you have spent it on a garment I will tear it up when I come, and if I don't know which it is I will tear them all up.'[307] Fortunately, his fears generally proved to be unfounded.

In the course of the years Martha was to show just how robust her constitution was. Not only did she have to cope with giving birth to six children in quick succession, but the large household with its young children and day-to-day chores also stretched her to her limits. On top of this came the many illnesses suffered by the children, which also took their toll on her and kept her on her toes as a nurse even at night: 'My poor Martha is leading a life full of harassments', wrote Sigmund.[308] While these were mainly common though contagious children's diseases, the life-threatening conditions of their eldest daughter Mathilde often gave cause for serious worry.

From time to time Martha too was subject to health problems, such as intestinal colic, migraine attacks and severe menstrual pains. Often she would not even stay in bed, but after the First World War, when her overall condition was weakened and she went down with pneumonia, her recovery was a more troublesome matter. Even after a two-week stay in a Salzburg sanatorium her exhaustion persisted, compounded by a chronic cough. To help her regain her strength, Helene Deutsch[309] would always bring goat's milk when she arrived for her analytic sessions at Berggasse 19.[310] Freud was anxious about his wife's worn-out condition, and especially worried about how to raise the money for her to be treated at a time when his income was being depleted by the country's inflation. It was not until the 1920s that Martha felt fully herself again. For a long time she was quick to tire, and even her summer stays at spas were not enough to heal her completely.[311]

A few years later, she was unwell again. In the summer of 1930 Martha arrived at their summer residence on the Grundlsee suffering from angina.[312] In January the following year a bout of influenza confined her to bed for a few days, which in view of her generally vigorous health warranted an entry in Freud's diary.[313] In the next few years her health was to give more frequent cause for concern, especially in 1933 and 1934, as emerges from Freud's correspondence.[314] Martha suffered from troublesome eczemas on her hands and feet, and was often unwell or run down, yet she firmly declined medical help. She was soon back on her feet, doing full credit to her reputation for resilience. Yet by the end of the 1930s, when she was in her late seventies, Martha was starting to acknowledge that she was not quite as young as she used to be: in February 1939 she wrote to a friend that she was gradually beginning to feel her age.[315] In spite of this gentle lament, she was still fit and active, unlike her sister, whose health was less stable.

The state of Sigmund's health, by contrast, was a much more serious worry to the family. Since 1923 he had suffered from oral cancer and had had to undergo more than thirty operations. First Freud had discovered a strange growth in his mouth, which struck him as abnormal when it proved persistent. A cursory preliminary investigation seemed to indicate a harmless superficial alteration of the mucous membrane that should be removed to be on the safe side. In April Freud asked Dr Felix Deutsch,[316] a friend and internist, to have a look at the lesion. Deutsch, who immediately saw that the supposedly benign leucoplakia was in fact a malignant tumour, advised him to have it excised without delay – though he did not mention the word cancer. Martha knew nothing of these consultations, Freud keeping quiet about the findings both to her and to the rest of the family. What was the point of unsettling them? He would go to an outpatient clinic, have the growth removed, and that would be that.

On the morning of the operation, Freud arrived at the clinic as arranged. Professor Marcus Hajek asked his famous patient to take a seat and loosen his tie a little. Freud was given a local anaesthetic, and Hajek got down to work. Yet as he cut the tissue away, his patient started bleeding more heavily than expected. With Freud swallowing blood and coughing, and more and more blood filling his mouth, the surgeon could no longer see what he was doing. The situation became critical. Hajek eventually succeeded in stemming the bleeding and was convinced that he had completely removed the growth. Having lost so much blood, Freud was kept on in the clinic after the operation and told to continue applying compresses to his wound. Martha and Anna were called, and to their dismay arrived at the clinic to find Sigmund slumped on a chair in his blood-splattered clothes after what had clearly been a highly dramatic operation – which neither wife nor daughter had even been told about! For further observation Freud was transferred to a room he shared with one other man, and Martha and Anna were told to go home and return at visiting time: the patient, they were assured, would be just fine. Yet before long

Freud suffered an attack of what turned into profuse bleeding that left him incapable of calling for assistance. His neighbour looked on in bewilderment before grasping the situation and rushing out for help. This was what saved Freud. Without his neighbour's timely intervention Freud would have possibly bled to death.[317]

୫ର

London

Emigration

Martha and Sigmund Freud lived for over forty years in the Berggasse. Freud's legendary love–hate relationship with Vienna has been the object of constant speculation. There were those, including his son Martin, who believed that his marked aversion to the city was just a way of concealing the true love he refused to acknowledge. In fact, Vienna did not always make things easy for him. Freud and his ideas met with intense disapproval there, and he had to assert himself in the face of considerable opposition. Perhaps, suggested Hanns Sachs, 'it was this opposition that made him find and choose for his future wife a girl who was decidedly not Viennese.'[1] Ever since his first trip to visit his half-brothers, Freud is likely to have felt more attracted to England than to Vienna. Descriptions of England, with its literature and culture, had fired his imagination from his early youth. He liked the mentality of the English, and from time to time even toyed with the idea of settling down on British soil. As fate would have it, it was here that he and his wife were to end their days.

At the beginning of 1938 the Freuds still felt safe in Vienna, even though Nazi Germany had long since cast its shadow over its neighbour Austria. Yet by mid-March Freud had given the country up for lost. 'Finis Austriae', he noted with resignation in his diary. The Wehrmacht had marched into Austria; German tanks, brown shirts and swastikas had suddenly imposed their presence upon the city's familiar streets; rejoicing supporters gave the National Socialists a rapturous welcome; cries of Heil Hitler! filled the air. Freud knew what this meant for Jews, yet he still failed or refused to see the consequences the Anschluss might also have for him and his family. In March 1938 a swastika appeared at Berggasse 19, and the Nazi emblem that fluttered conspicuously above the house entrance warned everyone who came that the times had changed dramatically.

One thing followed another. The premises of the psychoanalytical publishing house, the *Verlag*, were searched, and property, assets, the library and other materials were confiscated. The house telephone connection to Dorothy Burlingham's apartment, hitherto a merely practical arrangement, became the family's salvation. Should it come to another undesired 'visit', the housekeeper was instructed to slip away unobtrusively and make a quick, quiet phone call to Dorothy from the dining room. 'Then Mrs Burlingham will get help', Paula was told.[2] Their American friend had already arranged with the US Ambassador that if the SA or Gestapo were to return to their house she would ring up and one of the embassy staff would immediately come round on an ostensibly chance visit.

A group of armed SA men had burst in at Berggasse 19 almost immediately after the annexation, Martha finding herself face to face with the commando before she had even had time to collect her thoughts. A sentry remained at the door to ensure nobody escaped, while the others forced their way into the flat. Many people would have lost their cool at such a break-in, but Martha displayed remarkable courage. Far from showing her agitation, she is said to have approached the 'gentlemen' with frosty dignity and suggested they might wish to deposit their rifles in the umbrella stand for the duration of their visit. The money they demanded she handed over with the timelessly noble gesture of a generous hostess.[3] ' "Help yourselves", *Frau Professor* then said, as though it had been a bowl of dumplings.'[4] Yet their sinister visitors wanted more. Anna escorted them to the safe in another room and opened it. The booty from this lightning raid amounted to the equivalent of some US $840 or £300. Freud later commented wryly that this was more than he had ever taken for a single visit.[5]

A week later the Gestapo appeared looking for anti-Nazi documents. The flat was turned upside down, every last inch ransacked in search of incriminating papers. At the sight of one of the men on his way through the hall pausing at a large cupboard, pulling open its doors and starting to rummage through her piles of freshly laundered linen, Martha fearlessly confronted the shameless intruder, angrily ordering him to stop his impertinent behaviour at once. Her self-possession and intrepidity produced the desired result. Duly dressed down, the SS man withdrew and looked on in embarrassment as Martha set about piling the linen back in the cupboard. In the end, the Nazis found nothing worth confiscating and left. 'I think mother's attitude had had effect', said their son Martin.[6]

Yet this was not all. Escorted by a group of SS men, Anna was taken away for extensive questioning at the Gestapo headquarters on Morzinplatz. Like her brother Martin, she had long since been provided with Veronal capsules by the family doctor Max Schur in case it proved necessary to choose suicide over torture or concentration camps. Martin observed from the window as Anna was led to an open car. Her situation, as she was well aware, was perilous, but she showed neither fear nor particular concern, sitting there 'as a woman might sit in a taxi on her way to enjoy a shopping expedition'.[7] Her parents, by contrast, were quite overcome with anxiety and horror, unable either to oppose the Gestapo commanders or prevent the arrest. They could only speculate what the Nazis were planning to do with their daughter, and their fear and uncertainty were unbearable and unrelenting. Freud spent the whole day pacing the floor, smoking one cigar after another.[8] Endless hours passed before Anna eventually returned safe and sound. Whatever it was that she told the Gestapo about the scientific activities of the International Psychoanalytic Association, it seemed to her questioners innocuous enough for them to let her go again.

Yet now the die was cast. The agony of uncertainty, the all-pervading danger to life and limb, in the end made up Freud's mind for him. He now realized he had to leave Vienna. Struggling to keep his composure, he told his family of the inevitable decision. Friends had long since been urging him to leave, but without success. After all that had now happened, however, Freud no longer had a choice: at the last moment they had to abandon the sinking ship. England would welcome them with open arms.

Many others from their circles were in the same boat, other Jews whose lives were in just as much danger as Freud's own. Sigmund and Martha shared the fate of vast numbers of people who were persecuted and driven from the country by the Nazis. Yet they were so much luckier than most, who fell victim to the crime that was the 'Final Solution'.

In the time that remained, all activities were focused on leaving the country as quickly as possible, for time was short. A close colleague of Freud's arranged for a young photographer to come and take the final photos of Berggasse 19. On a grey morning in May 1938 Edmund Engelmann arrived at the house with his camera to hand and slowly worked his way through each room in the flat. Everything was still in its place: Freud's books, the antiquities he had collected, the famous couch. In a set of unique photographic documents Engelmann captured the memory of what had become a historic setting, one that would soon cease to exist in its present form.[9]

The weeks raced past dangerously quickly, yet the Freuds had no option but to bide their time. Every day Marie Bonaparte would keep watch over the door to their flat, crouching in the draughty stairway in her mink coat. Surely they would never dare detain a woman with a royal passport! Only after nearly three months spent living in fear did their waiting come to an end, following swift mediation by influential friends in international circles as well as endless red tape, harassment and bloody-mindedness on the part of the Nazis. This included paying the tax the authorities were vilely imposing on Jews for 'fleeing' the country – the *Reichsfluchtsteuer* – as well as the so-called Jewish property levy: after all, the regime had no intention of allowing its famous hostages to leave free of charge.

The last obstacles to them being given their exit visas seemed to have been overcome, and the Freuds finally received the necessary documents. Sigmund was required to give a receipt for the papers and sign a statement to the effect that he had been treated with due respect and consideration by the German authorities and in particular the Gestapo since the annexation of Austria by the German Reich. Freud did as he was told, but could not resist adding the ironic postscript: *Ich kann die Gestapo jedermann aufs beste empfehlen* – 'I can most highly recommend the Gestapo to everyone.' Fortunately, Freud's dig at the Nazis was without serious consequence. Furniture, pictures, antiquities, everything that had accumulated in the flat over the decades, was packed into boxes and made ready for the journey. What they left behind was an empty flat at Berggasse 19.

They were saved, but it proved impossible to get Freud's sisters to safety. Anna was the only sister to have emigrated, with her husband Eli Bernays, and had been living since 1892 in the United States. Four of Freud's sisters were forced to stay behind in Nazi Vienna: Regine Debora (Rosa), born in 1860 and married since 1896 to Heinrich Graf; Marie (Mitzi), born in 1861 and married since 1886 to Moritz Freud; Esther Adolfine (Dolfi), born in 1862 and unmarried; and Pauline Regina (Pauli), born in 1864 and married to Valentin Winternitz. All four were taken off to extermination camps in the early 1940s, and murdered by the Nazis.[10]

Refuge in Hampstead

Sigmund, Martha and Anna Freud left Vienna on 4 June 1938, accompanied by a small entourage that included both their loyal housekeeper Paula Fichtl and Dr Josephine Stross as Freud's personal physician. Other members of the family had already emigrated: on 5 May Minna had been the first to leave the country; Martin departed nine days later; Mathilde and her husband also left in May.[11]

They travelled west on the Orient Express, passing through Austria and southern Germany. That night they crossed the Rhine into France at Kehl, and were free. The journey continued as far as Paris, where they arrived exhausted next morning. At the station they were greeted by a group that included their son Ernst as well as Marie Bonaparte, who invited them to her house for the day. There Marie and her husband Prince George put on a small reception, also inviting Yvette Guilbert, who brightened up the dark times with her songs. Freud's little party then caught the night ferry over to England, and by next morning were at Dover, on English soil. It was the start of the final chapter in the life of Sigmund and Martha Freud, and London was to be the setting.

Paris, 1938: en route to London
From left to right: Annette Berman, Prince Waldemar of Denmark,
Anna, Josephine Stross, Marie Bonaparte, Sigmund Freud, Ernst,
Martha Freud, Prince George of Greece, Eugénie Bonaparte (?)

Arriving at Victoria Station, the exiles from Vienna were given
a fitting reception. After a temporary stay in rented accommodation
at 39 Elsworthy Road, at the end of the summer they moved to 20
Maresfield Gardens in the district of Hampstead, a large, red-brick

house covered with ivy, and with a pleasant garden shaded by trees. By now, the first furniture as well as Freud's collection of antiquities had arrived from Vienna, and they began to furnish the house. Their daughter Mathilde Hollitscher, who helped her mother with the housework, found a suitable flat close by. The area – a popular one with intellectuals, including a number of Germans[12] – soon became something of a Mecca for psychoanalysis, a home to 'the greatest gathering of psychoanalysts in the world'.[13]

It was here – where after his death the famous psychoanalytical centres were to come into being – that a now greatly weakened Freud found his final refuge. He had had to undergo a further operation, yet would still live to see the recognition of his work by important authorities. Martha, meanwhile, took pleasure in the public attention that was coming their way, informing her sisters-in-law in Vienna what an honour it was for the city to have 'our modest beloved old man in their midst'.[14] The newspapers had made them popular, indeed virtually turned them into stars. Letters addressed simply to 'Dr Freud, London' arrived without delay, and requests for autographs came fluttering into the house. Taxi drivers had learnt the route to 'Freud's place', and the manager at the local bank treated them courteously. The people in the shops where Martha was a customer – indeed, even passers-by on the streets – were quick to recognize their famous new neighbours and voice their support for them.[15] Not that these people had suddenly all been seized by enthusiasm for psychoanalytical doctrine. Rather, it was the circumstances – Freud's ill health, the flight of a renowned scholar from his native country, the new start he was making at such an advanced age – that aroused the general interest and induced a wave of affection and reverence for the prominent émigré and his family.

Martha was quickest to settle down in London. As Ernest Jones wrote, she never looked back towards Vienna but always straight ahead at what was new, as though she were twenty-seven instead of seventy-seven.[16] Three weeks after arriving in London she wrote to her niece Lilly Marlé: 'So far I have only been to two department stores and three parks, and I literally feel like a peasant coming to a city for the first time in his life. Everything is inconceivably big and splendid.'[17]

The actress Lilly Marlé (1888–1970), the daughter of Sigmund's sister Marie (Mitzi) and her husband Moritz Freud, a distant relative, is said to have been none other than 'Lili Marleen' from the famous song of the same name. The Hamburg poet Hans Leip, author of the words to the song, later recounted how he had come to write his haunting love poem in April 1915. He was on sentry duty at the Berlin barracks of the Guard Fusiliers on a cold and rainy night before leaving for the front: 'I was in love with two most respectable girls who were no older than I was, barely twenty. One of them, Lili, was an assistant in a greengrocer's. The other, Marleen, a doctor's daughter, was a nurse in a military hospital.'[18] That evening, Leip had sorrowfully bid farewell to the two of them, and he could not get either of them out of his mind. Scribbled down in a tiny notebook by the light of a street lamp, the three verses tell of separation and the presentiment of death. Leip dedicated it to both of the girls who had inspired it, Lili and Marleen. In 1938, twenty-three years after it had been written, the composer Norbert Schultze set Leip's words to music, and in spring 1941 the German forces radio station, *Radio Belgrad*, started playing the song, sung by Lale Andersen. It became an overnight success, and from then on went on the air every evening at ten o'clock. More and more European radio stations began to play the melancholy, wistful tune sung in a sensuous contralto voice. It moved the hearts of thousands of soldiers on both sides, Germans, French, English and Americans alike. It was both a glimmer of hope and an instrument of propaganda. Today it is a legend.[19]

Yet the actual origins of this international evergreen held more surprises in store. Anton W. Freud[20] claimed that Lilly, his first cousin once removed, had told him how the song had really come about. According to this account, Lilly had been friends with Hans Leip prior to her marriage to the actor Arnold Marlé in July 1918. In 1915 her affections had shifted from Leip to Marlé. Yet Leip dedicated his song to her, slightly disguising the name of his former girlfriend by adding 'en' at the end. Lilly had always maintained that she was Lili Marleen, but people only started to believe her once Hans Leip (1893–1983) himself conceded that he had known Lilly Marlé 'well'. If events really were as

Anton W. Freud portrayed them, the fact that so many loyal followers of Hitler were to sing a song about one of Sigmund and Martha Freud's nieces – and a Jewish girl at that! – takes on a specially grotesque light.

The Death of her Husband

Sigmund Freud had just a little over a year left to live after his move to London. Right through to the end, he struggled to keep on working and receiving visitors. As in Vienna, the Freud household was a place where friends of the family, famous contemporaries and artists came together. In July 1938 the Freuds entertained a young painter who had attracted considerable attention in the world of art and felt strongly influenced by Freud in his life and work. The Spaniard who asked to be allowed to sketch Freud struck his hosts as a rather droll, eccentric character: it was none other than Salvador Dalí.

In October 1938 Marie Bonaparte too paid them a visit, accompanied by her daughter Princess Eugénie.[21] Martha was not the only one who was happy to see their old friends. The others too were exceedingly excited about the visit. As Freud wrote, the princesses 'shared their time here between us, the Duke and Duchess of Kent, Queen Mary and their own king. All the girls in the house were very proud that they were with us for longest.'[22] Freud lived long enough to see Marie Bonaparte, his highly esteemed and invaluable friend, become a grandmother shortly afterwards.[23]

In January 1939 Sigmund and Martha invited the publisher Leonard Woolf and his wife Virginia, the writer, for tea at 20 Maresfield Gardens. Shortly afterwards H. G. Wells came to pay his respects. Yet the ailing Freud by now found such visits a strain. The eighty-three-year-old was visibly weaker, and by summer 1939 it was out of the question for him to continue working. Wrapped in blankets, he spent the warm days sitting in the quiet garden.

Freud, whose strength had long since left him, was in terrible pain. The secondary ulceration of his cancer wound had eaten a necrotic hole all the way through his cheek. The foetid smell of decomposing tissue was so strong that to Freud's great dismay even his beloved dog Lün would not go near him. He turned to his doctor for help, asking him to keep an old promise. Dr Max Schur, who had been the family doctor since he was a young man and understood the state of Freud's health better than anyone else, had made a pact with his famous patient: he would always tell Freud the truth and, when the time came, would not let him suffer unnecessarily. And keep his promise he did, not merely administering drugs to relieve the pain, but actually helping him to die.[24] After Schur had talked it over with Anna, for whom a final departure from her ailing father had hitherto been inconceivable but who was now called upon to make a decision, Freud was injected with morphine and fell into a twilight sleep. The women, Martha, Anna, Minna and Paula, and the doctors stayed with him during his final hours, waiting. Lux Freud wrote: 'All his children and Robert and I and Dr Schur and Dr Stross sat by him from Friday morning until Saturday at around midnight.'[25] Freud died in the early hours of 23 September 1939 without having regained consciousness. The family were comforted and cheered to know that he was now released from his suffering and had been true to himself right through to the end. His death did not come as a surprise: 'We had known since mid-September 1939 that Sigmund Freud was nearing his end. Friends [. . .] had been informed', wrote Arnold Zweig.[26]

In accordance with Freud's wishes, his body was cremated at Golders Green on the morning of 26 September, in a service attended by Martha, the family and a large gathering of mourners. His ashes were committed to an antique urn given to him by Marie Bonaparte. As ever, Martha Freud was gracious and concerned for others, behaving with the composure she expected from others too.[27] She kept this up over many weeks that followed, even though these were marked by the additional worry of her sister Minna's ill health. Writing to thank the many people who offered their condolences, she remarked that they would now have to live on without the goodness and wisdom of the man she had always referred to as 'Professor'. Yet she could not complain, she wrote in one letter, for she had been lucky enough 'to be able to look after him for more than one human lifetime, sparing him the

Martha and Sigmund Freud in Maresfield Gardens, 1939

everyday hardships of life',[28] a privilege for which she was extremely grateful. Yet now she missed him all the more. As she told her 'old friend' Margarethe Rie Nunberg, even though the children surrounded her with 'touching love', and she was receiving overwhelming testimonies of loyalty and devotion from all over the world, her life had 'lost its sense and meaning'.[29] Despite being a believer, she evidently did not feel 'sustained by a transcendent meaning' after her husband's death.[30] Even the recognition she was given for her role in Freud's private and professional life was cold comfort to her. At this point she still did not know what form her immediate future would take.

The first days after her husband's death Martha spent mainly sitting quietly in a chair in the drawing room. She preferred to be alone, and often spent the whole day in her room. Minna too, now in her late sixties and with a heart condition, hardly left her room any more. The loss of her 'idol'[31] had been a great blow to her. As time passed, Martha of necessity began focusing more on herself once again, and certain features of her personality re-emerged more clearly. On the first Friday after Sigmund's death she lit the Sabbath candles for the first time in half a century. Soon she was reading more again, though in her own defence she would point out that she of course only did so in the evenings. In her eyes, burying oneself in a book during the daytime – leisure, in other words – still had something slightly indecent about it, even when one was ninety years old. She would begin with her reading late in the afternoons, still preferring classical literature: she knew the same authors as her husband. Her grandson Anton W. Freud never forgot the sight of his grandmother sitting in a chair on the half-landing between the ground and the first floor at 20 Maresfield Gardens, reaching for a book from the shelf beneath the great window and staying there to read in the dim light, engrossed in her reading for hours on end.[32]

Anna, who had long since been giving her lectures on child psychology in English, resumed work at her practice just a few days after her father's death. Far from sinking into lethargy, *Fräulein Professor* positively threw herself into her work and resolutely seized the reins at the head of the psychoanalytical movement. She organized Freud's literary remains, prepared publication of the

Collected Papers, and sifted through thousands of letters and documents.

After the outbreak of war Anna – together with Dorothy Burlingham – turned her attention to new tasks. The two of them had already worked together in Vienna in the day nursery founded by the American Edith Jackson, which they ran from 1937 until it was shut down in March 1938. In London in the 1940s they built up the Hampstead War Nursery, a home for more than eighty children whose families had been broken up by the war. This was not only a psychoanalytically underpinned aid project, but at the same time a contribution to the struggle against Hitler and a token of gratitude for the reception they had been given in England. Philanthropists such as the Duchess of Kent, who was Marie Bonaparte's niece, Lady Lyons, who was the wife of the governor of the Isle of Wight, Lady Clarke and other influential figures helped finance Anna's project, and further funding came from contacts Dorothy had made in the United States.[33] Their first venture, planned for October 1940, provided temporary shelter for families who had been bombed out of their homes. Yet it emerged that there was a much greater need for accommodation for children who could not be evacuated without their mothers. In January 1941 the first wartime children's home was opened in Hampstead. To get her venture off the ground 'Miss Freud' had to find premises, negotiate for hours with officials and decision-makers, and undertake a tireless search for financial backing. She thus had little time left over for her mother, who for a long period succumbed to a crippling listlessness. Day-to-day matters were dealt with mainly by Anna and their devoted housekeeper Paula. The atmosphere in the house was very different from when Freud was alive.

The Second World War

It was not only Martha and the children, friends and relatives who suffered following Freud's death, but Paula too was deeply affected. Her loyalty to the Freuds remained unbroken, something the rest of the family never doubted, especially in the face of the troubled times that prevailed. After the first winter of war, the political situation deteriorated. In April 1940 the Germans occupied Denmark and Norway, and in May they invaded France. The British were expecting a parachute invasion by Hitler's troops at any moment. Fears of treachery in the country were on the increase, and scarcely a day passed by without xenophobic attacks in the popular press. Anti-German feelings ran high, stirring up mistrust of all refugees. Many foreigners were regarded as 'enemy aliens' until they could prove the contrary. Paula, whose 'move' to London had cost her her passport, was one of roughly 70,000 Germans and Austrians living in England without valid papers who represented a considerable security risk to the authorities. First lists of suspicious or potentially dangerous 'false' immigrants had been drawn up by English counter-intelligence as early as the summer of 1938. Hundreds of men and women were interned. The Home Office issued an order that all Germans over sixteen living in England were to be investigated for their trustworthiness. This went for Paula too. Her residence permit was assigned to category 'B' of the three categories of exiles, where 'A' signified dangerous and meant immediate internment, 'B' indicated dubious loyalty and entailed obligatory registration and travel restrictions, and 'C' referred to 'friendly' or 'genuine' refugees. Having left Austria of her own volition out of loyalty and devotion to the Freud family, Paula was on paper considered a potential threat: she was not Jewish, had no relatives in England but plenty in the enemy country, had not been forced to flee by the Gestapo, and furthermore had no desire to leave England again. As a result, she was unfortunate enough to be classified as 'not a refugee fleeing Nazi repression'.

When Hitler's armies flooded the continent early in 1940, British policy regarding foreigners was tightened up radically. The new government under Winston Churchill gave orders for every 'enemy alien' to be individually detained. Four days later, in mid-May 1940, there was a ring at the door of 20 Maresfield Gardens. Paula went to answer it. As she herself later recounted, a man identifying himself as a detective constable from Scotland Yard asked her whether she was Paula Fichtl and, when she duly replied, informed her that she would have to go with him.[34] The officer had instructions to take all 'B'-classified foreigners into custody. It was no good protesting, and neither Martha nor Anna Freud could do anything to help. An utterly bewildered Paula was told to pack together just her most essential requirements: it was only a temporary precaution they were taking. She was driven across the city in a police car, and before she had fully grasped what was going on they came to a halt in the courtyard of a women's prison. Her belongings were searched, and Paula – the supposed enemy alien – was taken to her cell. Hundreds of Austrians and Germans were to share a similar fate.[35] Ernst Freud too spent the summer of 1940 behind the barbed wire of a camp on the Isle of Man, while Martin was living in the most destitute of conditions as a prisoner near Liverpool.

At 20 Maresfield Gardens, meanwhile, everything possible was being done to bring the internments to an end. Anna addressed a petition to the Home Office and roped in all her English friends and acquaintances who were available, convinced they would be able to achieve something for Paula as well as her brothers. They wrote letters to higher authorities, assuring them that the internees could be trusted and did not present any threat, and even Lady Lilian Bowes Lyon, a cousin of Queen Elizabeth, wife of King George VI, submitted a request for the housekeeper's release. Yet it was to no avail. There was no prospect of Paula returning in the near future, and the Freuds would just have to do without her. This made life more difficult not only for Martha, but for the others as well. With the active support of the family housekeeper, they would have been better able to concentrate on the essential task of looking after the children, which was part of the war effort, so to speak, and of particular concern to Anna.

Fortunately they did find people who would help them: 'Mama cannot talk with them, but they somehow manage', wrote Anna.[36] August 1940 saw the start of the German bombing raids on southern England to prepare for the invasion. The first bombs fell on London, and more than sixty further attacks followed. 'Last night we had another visit from the bombs, but I stayed quietly in bed', wrote Martha in one communication to Paula.[37] Air-raid warnings soon became an everyday occurrence, and Martha told Paula how little she liked the sound the sirens made.[38] Yet having languished in apathy for so long after her husband's death, Martha now rose

Postcard to Paula Fichtl during her internment, 23 August 1940

Friday 23 Aug.

My dear Paula, yesterday received your kind letter from the 9th. The wishes you express for my next birthday, dear Paula, seem like a fairytale to me, for we have got used to thinking no further than the next day! The weather is already very autumnal here, and the blackouts now begin 2 minutes earlier every day. Last night we had another visit from the bombs, but I stayed quietly in bed. From Oli we had a telegram a few weeks ago saying that they had to leave Nice, now we don't know anything about them. Esti and Soferl also had to leave Paris, cycled further into France. Only the gods know when the whole family will be together again! Farewell dear Paula.

1000 greetings your M. F.

above herself: 'The nights are terrible, and in the morning one is surprised to find the house still standing and oneself still alive! I think you would hardly bear it: nerves of steel are called for.'[39] But this was just what Martha had. And so, 'fortunately', did the dog, who did not even stir at 'the rumble of gunfire'.[40]

Martha's letters to Paula Fichtl give an impression of the conditions under which people somehow had to battle on, conditions in which people had 'got used to thinking no further than the next day'.[41] She could take no pleasure, she wrote, in the 'most magnificent summer weather, with each day more beautiful than the one before', for 'the noise in the air' did not let up 'day or night'.[42] On account of the air raids, there were some nights when she 'did not even get out of her clothes'.[43] In one letter she described how in Fitzjohn's Avenue 'a bomb came down and destroyed a load of houses, the explosion was so big that one of the big panes of glass in the doors from Prof.'s room into the garden is completely shattered, as well as a few other windows'.[44]

As she wrote to Paula, 23 September was their 'sad day of remembrance',[45] the first anniversary of the death of their 'incomparable' Sigmund Freud.[46] Yet the war left them little time for commemoration. Everyday realities dictated the pace, and skill in improvisation became indispensable for getting by. In October the War Nursery began to operate, and Paula's help would have been more than welcome. Lady Lilian tried sending another petition, but again it was to no avail. Other 'B'-classified detainees were by now being released. Worse was to come, however. In January 1941 Minna had to be admitted to hospital. Her condition continued to deteriorate, and she lost consciousness and died in mid-February. Less than a year and a half after losing her husband, Martha had now lost the sister to whom she was so close, the only person to whom she could talk, as she put it, 'about my youth and everything we experienced together'.[47] After Minna's death Martha was often very lonely. At the same time, however, she had a great deal of work to do and many responsibilities that took her attention. She had no option but to rise to the challenge – and rise to it she did. Around the same time, Princess Marie Bonaparte, having learnt of Paula's seemingly never-ending internment, appealed directly to the prime minister Winston Churchill, and in spring

1941 Paula finally returned. But the situation had changed. The running of the household was back in the commanding hands of Martha Freud. In spite of the relentless passage of time, she had somehow kept going.

The Final Years

In the first winter after the war Martha – by now in her mid-eighties – still cut a sprightly figure. She supervised the gardener, went shopping every day, and endeavoured all round to maintain her sovereignty over domestic matters at 20 Maresfield Gardens. As usual, she read a good deal, wrote letters to friends, indulged her passion for handiwork, and wrote little poems to celebrate special occasions. Gradually people settled back into day-to-day normality. The children were well, and old friends she had not heard from for ages got back in touch, as people attempted to catch up with the fate or whereabouts of common acquaintances. Martha also tried to make Maresfield Gardens a home for the daughters of Freud's sisters.[48] It was some consolation to her to be able to help her nieces come to terms with the loss of their mothers in such appalling circumstances. A letter from the Red Cross had informed the family of the dreadful fate met by the four elderly women. As far as it had been possible to ascertain – details of the exact dates and circumstances of their deaths are contradictory[49] – they had all been killed in 1942, Marie in Theresienstadt, and Dolfi, Rosa and Pauline in the camps to which they had been transported after Theresienstadt. Later it emerged that Rosa had been murdered in Auschwitz and her two sisters in Treblinka.

Yet it was not only family contacts that were re-established, for the name of Freud had in the meantime taken on legendary status. Countless visitors wanted to pay their respects to *Frau Professor*, and Martha brought the glorious past back to life, enjoying both the pre-eminence achieved by her husband[50] and the kudos of being Sigmund Freud's widow. It had only now become clear that psychoanalysis was a broad scientific movement and not just a passing fad, and the fame associated with it was partly hers. Having previously always been so restrained, in her years of widowhood Martha struck many people as considerably more open and

approachable than when she was married.[51] She took an intense
interest in what was going on around her – sometimes too intense,
as her daughter Anna found to her dismay. From Anna's point of
view, her mother was not only too dominant around the house, but
also much too inquisitive about the patients who came up to her
consulting room.[52] It was in particular Anna's often well-known
adult patients who provided fodder for tittle-tattle, whereas the
child patients – unfortunately – gave much less cause for speculation and gossip. Though Anna refused to stand for any nonsense
where her practice was concerned, Martha seems not to have taken
the blessings of psychoanalysis as seriously as her husband or
daughter, and even child analysis was in her eyes far from sacrosanct. Even in Vienna Martha had already noticed the vast quanti-
ties of balls of wool and biscuits required during sessions, a
situation the young patients clearly took advantage of. The not
inconsiderable expenditure this entailed prompted Martha to make
the laconic comment: *Sie lässt sich's was kosten, die Kinderanalyse!*
('You'd be amazed what it costs, this child analysis!').[53]

It was not just the times that were changing: Martha herself had
changed. She continued to mourn for her husband and sister, but
it comforted her to know that she was not alone and many people
were concerned about her. She received all her visitors with the
same courtesy, charm and kindness, even when she sensed that
their main interest was in commemorating her husband and seeing
his final place of residence. Anna supported this tendency, setting
her father on a pedestal, as indeed Freud's own mother had done.
Maresfield Gardens (as well as Golders Green!) soon became
a place of pilgrimage for Freud's sundry followers. There was
a constant stream of friends, acquaintances, sympathizers and
representatives of the international analytical scene to the house,
not to mention their children. Martha took great pleasure in all
these visitors. She still attempted to manage domestic matters,
running the household together with Paula. The two of them can
have rarely been closer, especially since Anna was often away at
lectures and congresses or, whenever possible, at the cottage she
and Dorothy had bought in Walberswick as a replacement for
Hochrotherd, the house they had lost in Austria. Together Martha
and Paula would discuss the day's arrangements, the shopping, the

meals, and the catering for the guests. The selflessness with which Paula had become part of the Freud family over the past few decades was now particularly valuable to Martha, even if this did entail a moral obligation that was at times rather a burden. The two women were alike in their defining characteristics such as steadfastness, loyalty and a sense of duty, and in the final years of her life Martha clearly enjoyed having the familiar figure of Paula around her. Their life settled down into a regular groove – as far as this was possible given the continuing, indeed increasing, throngs of visitors to the house.

Martha soon found a further task too, acting as a repository of memories relating to Sigmund Freud. Biographers came to see her, and many other people approached her with questions. She assembled information and compiled family trees for the Freuds and the Bernays.[54] Yet although she enjoyed a full life and the affection of her children, Martha's world was becoming smaller and smaller. At the age of eighty-seven she wrote a letter to the seventy-year-old August Aichhorn – a long-standing friend of the family, who after the war reopened and ran the Vienna Psychoanalytic Society – in which she referred to herself as 'old mother Freud', an old grandma who rather innocuously still 'toddles around between children and children's children'.[55] Her humility and the pride she felt at her 'lack of obtrusiveness'[56] come clearly to light in this remarkable self-description, the self-assessment of a woman who had been brought up to regard tact, courtesy, restraint and self-sufficiency as the highest of virtues. In her own case, she had cause for satisfaction.

Martha's Death

When it came to the subject of death, Martha had a preference for the laconic. One of her favourite sayings was: 'one gets good soup when ill, and a good name when dead.'[57] Her husband, by contrast, had at an early stage begun thinking about the image that he and Martha would one day be leaving behind. In his mid-twenties, not long into their engagement, Sigmund was already imagining to himself how they would spend their life, as he put it, 'in silent happiness for us and serious activity for humanity, until

Eighty-sixth birthday, 26 July 1947
One of the last photographs

we must close our eyes to sleep our last sleep, and a memory of us lives on amongst our nearest and dearest in which everyone can only take pleasure.'[58]

In the summer of 1951 Martha's health deteriorated. Anna generally liked to spend the weekends at her cottage, where Martha and Paula could not impose their rules or curb her freedom,[59] but over these months she spent much of the time in London looking after her ninety-year-old mother, who had now become feeble and frail. Eventually Martha required home nursing, for which they hired Sophie Dann, who had previously cared for Martha's sister Minna and since 1945 had been working on a programme for war orphans.[60] As with Minna, Sophie dealt very capably with what was no easy task. By the final weeks Martha was no longer able to leave her bed. The wheel had turned full circle. At the end Martha lived entirely in the past, revisiting her youth and the glorious years at the side of her famous husband. Time and again she told her nurse of her beloved daughter Sophie, her little Sopherl, and how deeply and unceasingly she had mourned her. Shortly before she died on 2 November 1951, Martha called out 'Sophie, Sophie', and no one knew whether she meant her daughter or the nurse.[61]

At the funeral Anna asked a rabbi to give the oration, assuming that this would have been her mother's wish. Martha was cremated, her ashes were added to her husband's in the same Greek urn, and her name was chiselled under his in the stone column. Ernest Jones devoted a short obituary to her in the *International Journal of Psycho-Analysis*. Paula wrote in her notebook: '6 o'clock in the evening my dear good Frau Professor is dead one of my hardest days in my life She was love and goodness itself, no one can replace her. 5 nov funeral.'[62]

Her death was a painful loss for the children. Otherwise so restrained, especially in her relationship with her mother, Anna was on this occasion distraught. When she rang one of her patients to call a session off, a rarity in itself, she broke down in tears on the phone – to the patient's utter surprise.[63] The baby of the family had now come of age once and for all. However, Martha's death also represented something of a release for Anna, for her relationship to her mother, though outwardly amicable, had always been fraught with conflict on an emotional level.[64] One immediate change was to the domestic structure. Dorothy Burlingham, who until Minna's death in 1941 had lived in a flat at 2 Maresfield Gardens,[65] was now finally able to lead a shared life with Anna. The house at 20 Maresfield Gardens was big enough for Dorothy to invite her children and grandchildren to visit, and the two women also bought a larger house in Walberswick.[66] At the age of fifty-six, Anna was now for the first time 'a partner in her own household'.[67] This arrangement clearly made it easier for Anna to find peace of mind, and outwardly too she began to show a gentler side.[68]

Anna's relationship with her mother has remained in many respects a mystery. As a daughter she had shut her eyes to any identification with Martha, and she hardly came to grips with this as an analyst either. She made particularly heavy weather of admitting that she in some way needed her mother.[69] Was it not the father, after all, around whom everything revolved? Freud himself, who had always given more thought to his father and unconsciously tried to leave certain aspects of his ambivalence towards his mother unanalysed, claimed that the father's death was the most deeply distressing experience in a man's life, a more decisive loss than that of the mother.[70]

Anna tried to reconcile herself to the contradictions in her conception of Martha and draw a line under the tensions of the past. This allowed her to recognize her mother's qualities and explicitly acknowledge the high regard in which she held her. Only now was she able to admit the respect Martha had inspired in her, the admiration she felt for her fortitude and fearlessness. The spirit her mother had shown during the emigration had made a particularly lasting impression upon her, and she would often tell Dorothy's daughters and granddaughters how resolutely Martha had faced the Nazi soldiers, how she had adjusted herself to all requirements and risen to all challenges.[71] Answering the condolences that came to Maresfield Gardens from all over the world, Anna's more official letters in particular made no bones about portraying her mother – who had enjoyed the 'privilege' of being her father's companion through life, his *Lebensgefährtin* – as a historic figure.[72]

A measure of Martha's importance as Sigmund Freud's *Lebensgefährtin* is that her death was to be of direct consequence for Freud research, for only after she died did it become possible to see Sigmund's many love letters to Martha. It was Ernest Jones who was granted the privilege of access to the roughly 1,500 letters Martha had kept.[73] According to their son Martin, none of the children except Anna had ever wanted to read them, regarding them as 'much too sacred'.[74] After her husband's death, Martha had repeatedly said that she was going to burn the letters, and it was only at her daughters' request that she refrained from doing so.[75] A good job too. Martha's letters display style, refinement, etiquette, and what Paul Roazen has described as a high degree of

Anna and Sigmund Freud

classical Viennese tact[76] – a verdict that would have delighted Martha.

Reading the letters gave Anna her first contact with the past her parents had shared, and aroused her jealousy with respect to the times she had not been part of. Yet she soon became so immersed in the passion exhibited by their correspondence that she found herself able to relate to her mother in a way that unleashed many positive feelings towards her.[77] What she recognized and valued above all was Martha's determination and strength of character. Even today, however, there are persistent rumours that Anna manipulated the image of her parents by destroying a lot of the letters, especially Martha's. She was considered a tough censor. On the one hand, she was justifiably eager to prevent excessively intimate matters from being made public. On the other hand, she was keen to influence the idea people formed both of psychoanalysis and her parents.

Martha and her Influence on Psychoanalysis

'I must admit that if I did not realize how seriously my husband takes his treatments, I should think that psychoanalysis is a form of pornography', René Laforgue reported Martha Freud once saying to him.[78] To her mind there was something vulgar about psychoanalysis, something from which she dissociated herself. Marie Bonaparte described how Martha had once told her how much her husband's work had surprised and even upset her in its permissive treatment of sexuality, claiming that she had almost intentionally refused to become acquainted with it. Freud had replied that his wife was simply 'very bourgeoise'.[79]

To say that the new method meant nothing to Martha is only half the truth. Clearly the Freuds' marriage was not a work-based intellectual association between two equal partners. After all, Martha had no psychoanalytical training, and her interest in the field was strictly limited. Active commitment on her part seems scarcely to have gone beyond occasional assistance, for example when it came to forwarding manuscript proof corrections.[80] Although she was uninterested in the details, however, psychoanalysis was not a closed book to Martha. Her ignorance was probably only feigned, indeed cultivated as part of a pre-arranged division of labour with her husband, each of them letting the other one be. It certainly made matters easier for Freud that he never heard a word of doubt from his wife concerning his unorthodox methods of treatment.[81] Conversely, it was perhaps only thanks to her feigned ignorance that Martha was able to live with what she viewed as the dubious field of her husband's activity. Yet Martha's uncompromisingly bourgeois mentality may well in fact have lent support to the whole psychoanalytic movement. One may ask whether Freud would have been as successful at convincing the upper echelons of the establishment of the seriousness of his method if he had not had the background he did, which included his status as a married man with a solid middle-class home. From others at the time such bold advances may well have been considered even less forgivable. Nevertheless, Freud's bourgeois way of life was not just a matter of style and by no means a merely feigned or strategic position from which he could be all the more provocative in his work. It was precisely his conservative lifestyle that provided the support and gave him the courage to go beyond customary limits and overthrow accepted norms.

Freud may have also benefited from his relationship with Martha in another way. As she hardly came into direct contact with the professional order of psychoanalysis and clearly belonged to 'another world', there was a sense in which she was also immune to the unpleasant sides of psychoanalytical insight. Freud, who was after a general psychology with which to explain the workings of the mind, was able to see in Martha someone who stood apart from what he learnt about humankind in general. In these terms, she was far removed from the depths of the human soul, depths with which Freud – 'a pessimist about human nature'[82] – had more frequent encounters than he would have liked. Since mankind on the whole was in Freud's eyes a *Gesindel* or 'rabble', Oskar Pfister put it in a letter to Martha, 'he needed you all the more, and without you even this giant would not have been capable of the enormous achievement that has been bestowed upon "good-for-nothing" mankind through his life's work.'[83] Freud did not wish to share the blackest depths of his knowledge with Martha, but rather to protect her from them.

What is certain is that, for all the distance she kept, Martha naturally regarded her husband's field of investigation as important. She was aware that (hysterical) pathologies existed for which traditional medical treatments were inadequate, and that it was thanks to Freud that new and effective ways in neurology had been found for helping in such situations. In the early days at least, he would tell her of his 'strange case histories'[84] such as the one involving her friend Bertha Pappenheim, although in this particular case he preferred to wait until they were married before revealing the shocking details. For Martha it was obvious anyway that only something unspeakable could have induced Breuer to break off his treatment in so abrupt a manner, and she understood that this something must have been sexual in nature.[85]

There can be no doubt either that once they were married, if not before, Martha followed her husband's daily working routine with the greatest possible attention – as he followed hers. In his magnum opus *The Interpretation of Dreams* (1900) he made use of Martha's dreams, fears, ailments and afflictions to draw conclusions from which psychoanalytical ideas were to emerge. It was 'the dream of Irma's injection', a product of his relationship with

Martha, that showed the direction his future work was to take and revealed to him the secret of the unconscious and wish-fulfilment through dreams: shortly before her thirty-fourth birthday on 26 July 1895, Martha had told her husband of the plans for the day and the guests she was expecting, and during the night of 23 July Sigmund took up this announcement of Martha's in his dream about Irma's injection. The dream is set in a large hall, in which they are receiving their many guests. Freud takes 'Irma' to one side, recognizing her as a friend of the family and one of his patients, and reproaches her for not having accepted his 'solution'. If she still has pains, he tells her, this is really just her own fault. Irma replies that the pains in her throat and stomach are more severe than he realizes. Worried, Freud looks down her throat, and sees whitish scabs. Other doctor friends now appear in the dream, and it somehow emerges that it is these other doctors who are responsible for Irma's pains. His friend Oscar Rie has thoughtlessly given Irma an injection with something like propionic acid, and probably – Freud surmises – the syringe was not clean either. In July 1895, when Freud had this dream, Martha was three months pregnant. Among other things, Freud interpreted his dream as a wish not to be to blame for Martha's stomach pains, in other words their unwanted pregnancy.[86]

The Interpretation of Dreams was not the first of Freud's writings on which Martha had left her mark. Her imprint is present in earlier works as well. When in the 1890s he reflected on the torments of sexuality attendant upon modern life, he was writing in large measure about himself. During his engagement, his highly charged emotions, his impatience and his impetuous love had all been focused upon a single faraway object: Martha. Freud extrapolated from his own tortured experience of unfulfilled desire and assumed that others too would suffer from the consequences when gratification was deferred. Freud's wait for Martha thus served as a model in his work on the aetiology of neuroses.[87]

Freud held a number of the women around him in high regard as scientists or artists, which was in itself far from being a foregone conclusion given that – among other things – he regarded women as having less energy for sublimation as a result of their lower libido. Nonetheless, he believed that a woman's true place was in the home, bringing up the children. It cannot be ruled out that he constructed this image of woman in order to defend himself from an intense fear of women produced by his emotional dependence upon his mother, and that he extended this dependence to Martha.[88] Certainly, he was afraid of being left by Martha;[89] he laid exclusive claim to her and needed her enormously. On the receiving end of his flood of letters, she played a role similar to the one Wilhelm Fliess would assume once they had married. Just as Sigmund analysed his own feelings in his letters to Martha, so he combed through her letters to him with an attention to detail 'worthy of a detective – or a psychoanalyst'.[90] With both his wife and later his friend Fliess, he shared his innermost feelings and reflections and laid bare his most intimate thoughts. While it was just the two of them before they had children, Martha was Freud's most important source of emotional stability: whenever he was down or received a setback, it was Martha who made up for everything.[91]

As Martha gave her attention increasingly to the children, this post became vacant,[92] and Freud found a substitute in Wilhelm Fliess. As he wrote in one letter to him, 'In my life, as you know, woman has never replaced the comrade, the friend.'[93] The two men had first met in autumn 1887, when Fliess visited Vienna as part of his training. On Breuer's advice, Fliess attended some of Freud's lectures on neurology, and once he was back in Berlin in November he received a letter from Freud expressing in the most heartfelt of terms his desire that they should pursue their acquaintance further. The tone and style of even this first letter – formal, yet at the same time fervent – was different from what was customary in Freud,[94] possibly hinting at the unique character of the friendship that would bind the two men for many years. This led to a change in his relationship with Martha, which is unlikely to have gone unnoticed on her part. The lively exchange of ideas with Fliess gave Freud the emotional and intellectual confidence gradually to develop his own psychology. In dealing with him, Freud had no need to mince words and feared neither ridicule nor hostility. Their intimate correspondence and their meetings in person, which they called 'congresses', created a protective space that made it possible for Freud to face his personal and professional problems self-analytically. Whereas with his wife he kept quiet about his worrying physical disorders such as chest pains and arrhythmia, here too he confided in Fliess. Freud idealized his friend beyond all measure, and it was only gradually that he began to see through his own 'transference' and recognize the 'true' Fliess with his mysticism and his obsessive fixation on the all-pervasive power of numerology.[95] Eventually their relationship was severed, ending up in acrimony and mutual recriminations.[96] The emotions aroused had been too complex; their viewpoints too incompatible; their attacks on one another too fierce. They met for the last time in 1900.

Freud's correspondences with both Martha and Fliess testify to a high degree of introspection on his part. Freud's behaviour resembled an analysand's towards his analyst. Under Fliess's influence he completed his self-analysis, writing as though he only really came to life with pen to hand. Such personal letter-writing was something of a safety valve for Freud: it mobilized creative energies and structured his thoughts like a process of catharsis or meditation.[97] Martha herself functioned as an incubator for Freud's as yet embryonic ideas, a silent 'other' to whom he could address his monologues. This impression is corroborated by the fact that so far only Freud's letters to Martha have been published, and not – apart from a few exceptions – her replies to him, a reflection of the asymmetrical relationship between the patient who tells and the analyst who listens. In writing his letters, Freud summoned Martha before his mind's eye, yet like an analyst she was outside his field of vision. She provided him with space for fantasies, but responded only sporadically as a result of her physical distance. Moreover, her generally reticent, restrained manner, her attentiveness, loyalty and patience, as well as her ability to immerse herself in his world while at the same time keeping a grip on her own, were in many respects comparable with the attitude of an analyst. He gave vent to intense emotions; she did not (and at times he even felt she was rather cool). He associated freely, judging it his task not to gloss over anything and to be honest at all costs; she kept her eye on reality and insistently brought him back down to earth. With and through Martha, Freud tried and tested over a protracted period what he was to finish off with

Fliess. As Wilhelm Salber wrote,[98] Martha was the first student in Freudian psychology.

Martha not only influenced her husband's writings, but was also the source of impulses that come to light in the work of Anna Freud. Sigmund gave his youngest daughter her first introduction to psychoanalysis when she was fourteen years old. It took the form of a mysterious lesson imparted during the course of an evening stroll past the beautiful villas near the Prater in Vienna. Pointing at the buildings, Freud said: 'You see those houses with their lovely façades? Things are not necessarily so lovely behind the façades. And so it is with human beings too.'[99] He fostered Anna's interest in his work, and encouraged her to make psycho-analysis her own area of study and become his training analysand, considering it a suitable occupation for a woman. This was to have a number of repercussions, not limited solely to the consequences of the direct transmission of views from father to daughter or the effects that their analytical alliance would have upon their real-life, private relationship. It can be surmised that deep-seated prob-lems and objections on Anna's part could not be voiced within this arrangement and remained unanalysed.[100] In her father's writings, however, it was perfectly possible for Anna to come across more or less coded material from their sessions. She could 'read Freud', in other words, in order to find out about herself and what her father thought (about her).

One consequence of the blind spots in her self-knowledge to which the setting was conducive – her 'unresolved father-complex'[101] – was Anna's failure to recognize or work through her patients' Oedipal entanglements. Though she later modified her stance, the early Anna believed that child analysis, unlike adult treatment, required a special, non-analytic introductory phase in which the child's trust was built up as the basis for future processes of transference.[102] The value of this approach was that it made it easier to control hostile, dismissive or provocative behaviour on the part of the children, but the drawback was that it hindered the analytic study of aggression and negative transference. The emphasis Anna laid on positive transference in child analysis reflected her own reluctance to express negative feelings towards her father.[103] The difficulty she had acknowledging such unpleasant emotions in her own case was bound to have an effect on her dealings with others too.

But where did the mother stand in relation to this father-fixation? Martha exerted a great influence upon Anna's motivations. Anna was a qualified teacher and the founder of child psychoanalysis, in other words someone who was surrounded by children, who guided them, instructed them and knew how to treat them 'better' than their own parents or mothers did. Research on the psychodynamics of women who have chosen a job involving looking after other people's children – whether as infant nurses, nannies or teachers – has suggested that many such professional childminders themselves as children often felt rejected or excluded by their mother. Identifying with the children in their care, they now want to be a better, more understanding mother to them, and frequently feel superior to their charges' real mothers.[104] By the same token, Anna Freud's choice of profession presumably had its roots not only in her idealization of her father and dependence upon him, but also in her specific relationship with her mother. Certainly, she derived her later empathy with children in part from her memory of the at times bitter pain she experienced during her childhood and her feeling of being left out, alone, and a bore to the others.[105]

Anna devoted intensive attention to Oedipal themes, moreover, and disregarded the special significance of the mother–child relationship for longer than other analysts. In her case studies it was the father who was the most important character,[106] as though she was out to deny the mother's existence. Possible parallels with the figure of the mother or father in her own life are patent. On a psychological level she tried to ignore the mother – the better to be able to apotheosize the father, according to Elisabeth Young-Bruehl. Anna was almost compelled to behave in this way, so intense were her feelings of rage, envy and jealousy towards her mother. After Martha's death, there was a change in Anna Freud's theoretical interests. In her lectures on male homosexuality, for example, she now also turned her attention to the child's devotion to the mother.[107] It can be no coincidence that it was in the year her mother died that her thoughts took this turn. Although she did not find it easy to acknowledge her bonds with her mother, it became increasingly clear how far her ideas on motherhood were shaped by Martha's influence and how this found expression in her own psychoanalytical work.[108]

Martha Freud: an Epilogue

Martha Bernays-Freud was a witness to a whole era. She lived through key moments of history, accompanying through life the man and myth-maker Sigmund Freud, who left his mark on the last century and recent past as few others have done. Their shared path brought her into contact with many significant figures from the worlds of science, art and public life, and Martha formed part of a circle that wrote cultural history. Right from the engagement and marriage that took place against her mother's will, Martha stood by her husband in the face of all opposition, imperturbable even when he was being fiercely attacked and ostracized by official science for his scandalous views. When Freud felt isolated and believed he was on an imaginary blacklist, Martha remained impervious to all doubt. Her equanimity and strength of character proved vital to both of them in many an extremity.

Without ever cultivating the posture of a prima donna, in the early years of their relationship in particular Martha was her husband's 'muse', his solace and refuge. Martha herself and Freud's relationship to her – with the image he had of her – spurred him to pursue intellectual games and self-reflections, galvanized him into forming new ideas, and inspired dreams that took him forward in his research work. It was not through the cooperation of a kindred spirit but through her composure and support that she strengthened Freud in the opinions and ambitions that were to lead to psychoanalysis. Their love was passionate and extreme, provoking the most intense of reactions, yet Martha kept her feet firmly on the ground. Her task was to protect the man and later the family from external crises and disturbances so that he could devote his time and energy fully to research and writing.[109]

Martha Freud complied with the conventional expectations of a bourgeois wife of the nineteenth and early twentieth centuries,[110] providing her husband with emotional stability and practical support and sparing him the irksome trivialities of life. We cannot know just how much self-denial this attitude required, yet her education, early experiences and strict religious commitment are likely to have helped her fulfil her self-imposed task. She was always there and never in the way. 'My mother believed in my father, not in psychoanalysis', wrote Anna Freud.[111]

Decisively shaped by the conventional moral notions of the day, Martha Freud nonetheless proved to be surprisingly open-minded and pragmatic, guided as she was by a sense of responsibility towards others.[112] Her philanthropic integrity was unshakable. The guidelines she followed were not the rigid dictates of some strict moral code: rather, she formed her views according to what seemed human in each particular case. When it came to herself, she was a strict judge. Martha Freud seems to have been willing and resolved to do and endure anything that destiny might require of her. The expectations of those around her seem hardly ever to have come into conflict with her own, and she gave the impression of being at one with herself. This attitude, as well as the fitting circumstances in which she found herself, made it natural for her to accept her role. Succeeding in this was a source of pride and fulfilment to her. What might have appeared to be passivity, weakness and subservience were in her eyes activity, strength and sovereignty.

Chronological Table

1860 Birth of brother Eli (Elias) Bernays.
1861 Martha Bernays is born in Hamburg on 26 July, the daughter of Berman and Emmeline Bernays.
1865 Birth of sister Minna.
1869 The family moves to Vienna.
1872 Death of brother Isaac (born 1855).
1879 Death of father on 9 December.
1882 Engagement to Sigmund Freud in Vienna, summer holidays in Wandsbek. Freud reconsiders his professional career and starts work at Vienna General Hospital.
1883 Martha moves to Wandsbek with her mother and sister.
1886 Freud founds his practice. Martha marries Sigmund Freud in Wandsbek and moves back to Vienna.
1887 Birth of daughter Mathilde on 16 October (died 20 February 1978).
1889 Birth of son Jean Martin on 7 December (died 25 April 1967).
1891 Birth of son Oliver on 19 February (died 24 January 1969). The Freuds move into Berggasse 19.
1892 Birth of son Ernst on 6 April (died 7 April 1970).
1893 Birth of daughter Sophie on 12 April (died 25 January 1920).
1895 Birth of daughter Anna on 3 December (died 9 October 1982).
1896 Martha suffers from 'writing paralysis'. Minna moves in with her sister's family once and for all.
1899 *The Interpretation of Dreams*, Freud's most important book, appears in November.
1902 Martha's husband is appointed professor. Establishment of the Wednesday Psychological Society at Berggasse 19.
1908 Berlin gradually turns into the new focal point of their psychoanalytical and private affairs.
1910 Death of mother on 26 October. Psychoanalysis continues to flourish and spread.
1914 The Freud sons sign up for military service in the First World War.
1920 Death of daughter Sophie in Hamburg in January. From 1920 onwards Ernst and Oliver found families in Berlin.

1923   Sigmund falls ill with cancer. Death of grandson Heinerle on 19 June and brother Eli on 12 October.

1938   Psychoanalysis and its founders are at the peak of their popularity. Emigration to London in early June.

1939   Death of husband on 23 September. Outbreak of Second World War.

1940   Internment of family members as 'enemy aliens'.

1941   Death of sister in February.

1945   Post-war fame as Sigmund Freud's widow. Freud's doctrines are institutionalized worldwide.

1951   Death of Martha Freud on 2 November.

Notes

1 Schütt (1997) 234.
2 A. W. Freud (2001).
3 Louven (1991b) 250.
4 Kopitzsch and Tilgner (1998) 172.
5 Cf. E. Duckesz (1907), 'Zur Biographie des Chacham Issak Bernays'. In *Jahrbuch der Jüdischen Literarischen Gesellschaft*, vol. 5, quoted in STAH, Genealogical Collection 1.
6 Jones (1954), vol. I, 128.
7 Ibid.
8 Louven (1991b) 250.
9 Cf. STAH, Genealogical Collection 1.
10 Louven (1991a) 99.
11 STAH, Genealogical Collection 1.
12 Hamburg City Directory 1876, p. 38.
13 From 1865 to 1867 the family rented accommodation on the second floor of Mühlenstrasse 38. The landlord, who lived on the ground floor, was the Jewish merchant Anton Baruch. The basement was a fruit and vegetable shop. From 1867 to 1868 the Bernays lived in the district of St Pauli, at Carolinenstrasse 2. The landlord here was the master bricklayer J. P. Schuldt. Finally, from 1868 to 1869 the Bernays lived at Glashüttenstrasse 34, in a house likewise owned by Schuldt. The bricklayer lived on the ground floor (STAH, Genealogical Collection 1).
14 Louven (1991b) 251.
15 STAH, detention entry in prison administration records, C11, vol. 5, registration no. 130.
16 STAH, Commercial Court B 1, no. 4291, Bankruptcy and accompanying files/criminal investigation files.
17 STAH, Genealogical Collection 1, records of the court proceedings.
18 STAH, Genealogical Collection 1.
19 Lange (1986), table II a, commentary p. 41. (Some sources give 1868 as the date of the removal.)

20 STAH, Genealogical Collection 1, Haasenstein & Vogler to Berman Bernays, 29 January 1869.
21 Jones (1954), vol. I, 112.
22 STAH, Genealogical Collection 1.
23 Rabadán de Ayala (1998).
24 Ibid.
25 STAH, Genealogical Collection 1, Communication from the Archive Administration of Vienna City Council, 13 March 1961.
26 STAH, Genealogical Collection 1, records of the court proceedings, verdict of exoneration.
27 Appignanesi and Forrester (1992) 81.
28 STAH, Authority for guardianship, records of guardianship cases, 1882, Series III, no. 1399.
29 Sachs (1944) 21.
30 One of the daughters of Martha's uncle Elias (1824–98), Egla-Elsa, born in Wandsbek in 1879, was also married to a Max Halberstadt, born in 1872 in Hamburg, the son of Samuel Halberstadt and Henriette Heymann (cf. the Bernays Family Tree, A. W. Freud (2002)).
31 Gillis-Carlebach (2000) 15.
32 Sigmund Freud to Marie Freud, 20 July 1912.
33 Cf. Gillis-Carlebach (2000) 377 (family tree). Gillis-Carlebach's grandmother, Martha-Rachel Halberstadt (1876–1960), was one of Max Halberstadt's sisters.
34 Gillis-Carlebach (2000) 15.
35 Sigmund Freud (1992) 71.
36 STAH, Alphabetical registration index, Alt-Hamburg 1892–1925, excerpt 332–8, registration system A 30.
37 Jones (1955), vol. II.
38 Resident at Parkallee 18 (Hamburg City Directory 1919).
39 STAH, Alphabetical registration index, Alt-Hamburg 1892–1925, excerpt 332–8, registration system A 30.
40 Gay (1988) 391.
41 Freud to Sándor Ferenczi, 4 February 1920.
42 Heinz Rudolf Halberstadt (1918–23), known as Heinerle (cf. Jones) or Heinele (cf. Gay).
43 W. E. Freud (2000). This latter was regarded as the best-known progressive school in Hamburg during the Weimar Republic. Closed in 1937 by the National Socialists, it was conceived as a 'school of culture' with high pedagogical and artistic standards. (Cf. Kopitzsch and Tilgner (1998) 302.)
44 W. E. Freud (2000).
45 STAH, Genealogical Collection for Halberstadt, Certificate of the Public Information and Advice Centre for Emigrants in Hamburg, 24 February 1936.

46 Sigmund Freud (1992) 197.
47 Also written Isaak. This option was also possible in the case of Martha's brother Isaac.
48 Kopitzsch and Brietzke (2001) 44.
49 Ibid.
50 *Jewish Encyclopaedia*, 1902, cited in Lange (1986).
51 Kopitzsch and Brietzke (2001) 44.
52 M. Freud (1957) 13.
53 Kopitzsch and Brietzke (2001) 44.
54 Bernays worked at the Kohlhöfen Synagogue (no longer in existence). For a time, he was also registered in the street of the same name, at numbers 90 and 267, until he moved to Elbstrasse 21 in 1835 (Hamburg City Directory 1824–45).
55 Kopitzsch and Brietzke (2001) 45.
56 Ibid.
57 Schütt (1997) 267.
58 Lange (1986), table II a, commentary p. 37.
59 Kopitzsch and Brietzke (2001) 45.
60 Ibid.
61 Ibid.
62 Ibid.
63 Lange (1986), table II a, commentary p. 37.
64 Jones (1954), vol. I, 112.
65 Lange (1986), table I.
66 Jones (1954), vol. I, 112–13.
67 Lange (1986), table II a, commentary pp. 37 and 42.
68 Theweleit (1994) 42ff.
69 Berman Bernays for a time lived at Pelzerstrasse 23 (Hamburg City Directory 1856). His mother, 'Widow Isaac Bernays', was in 1856 registered at the Hopfenmarkt, and before that at Ellernthorsbrücke no. 9 (Hamburg City Directory 1851).
70 Louis (Juda) Bernays, whose real name was Lewin Bernays, applied to change his first name – or, to put it more precisely, he applied for additional French first names for his wife, his children and himself – by way of preparation for the family's move to Paris. The change was granted by the Hamburg Senate on 12 March 1877 (STAH, Genealogical Collection 1).
71 Lange (1986), table II a, commentary p. 41.
72 A. W. Freud (2002).
73 Ibid.
74 Theweleit (1994) 51.
75 Ibid. Freud's half-brothers Emanuel (1833–1914) and Philipp (1834–1911) stemmed from his father Jacob's first marriage to Sally Kanner.

76 Gay (1988) 8.
77 Krüll (1979).
78 Ibid.
79 M. Freud (1957) 35.
80 A. W. Freud (2002).
81 M. Freud (1957) 35.
82 Bernays Family Tree, A. W. Freud. Minna Ruben's father was called Elias ben Ruben (1749–1822). He was married twice. Minna was born from the second marriage with Egla Stern, who was the daughter of Hertz Stern and Hitza Hirsch and after whom Martha's mother was named. This lineage again shows the extent of Martha's family's Jewish roots, which went back generations.
83 STAH, Genealogical Collection 1.
84 It is unclear whether Mary was related to Heinrich Heine, although this is generally doubted. All that is known is the name of her parents, Julius Heine and Sophie Friedberg (Bernays Family Tree, A. W. Freud).
85 Isaac-Oscar likewise lived in London when the Freuds emigrated there decades later (A. W. Freud (2002)).
86 M. Freud (1957) 13–14.
87 Ibid., 14.
88 Freud to Martha Bernays, 6 September 1882, cited in Jones (1954), vol. I, 128.
89 Jones (1954), vol. I, 134.
90 Ibid., 129.
91 Freud to Minna Bernays, 21 February 1883.
92 M. Freud (1957) 14.
93 A. W. Freud (2002).
94 Freud to Martha Bernays, 15 November 1883.
95 It is uncertain whether Freud was here alluding to Martha's family history. What is beyond doubt is that in the novel a 'Martha' plays a significant role in the protagonist's life.
96 Freud to Martha Bernays, 22 August 1883.
97 Freud to Martha Bernays, 16 December 1883.
98 Jones (1954), vol. I, 77.
99 Gay (1988) 40.
100 Jones (1954), vol. I, 113.
101 Gay (1988) 40.
102 Jones (1954), vol. I, 127.
103 Ibid., 123.
104 Ibid., 125.
105 Gay (1988) 41.
106 Freud to Martha Bernays, 3 August 1882, quoted in Jones (1954), vol. I, 113.
107 Freud to Martha Bernays, 15 March 1884, quoted ibid.

108 Freud to Martha Bernays, 21 April 1884.
109 Jones (1954), vol. I, 133.
110 Freud to Martha Bernays, 6 July 1885.
111 Freud to Martha Bernays, 8 November 1885.
112 Freud to Martha Bernays, 8 September 1883.
113 Stephan (1992) 26.
114 Ibid., 30.
115 Freud to Martha Bernays, 30 June 1884.
116 Ibid.
117 Jones (1954), vol. I, 122.
118 Young-Bruehl (1989) 38.
119 Ibid., 308.
120 Tichy and Zwettler-Otte (1999) 58.
121 Brecht, Friedrich et al. (1992).
122 Freud to Martha Bernays, 26 June 1885.
123 Jones (1954), vol. I, 115.
124 Ibid.
125 Ibid.
126 Ibid.
127 Ibid., 116.
128 Ibid., 120.
129 Freud to Martha Bernays, 15 June 1882.
130 Jones (1954), vol. I, 119.
131 Ibid., 120.
132 Ibid., 121.
133 Gay (1988) 37.
134 Ibid., 10.
135 Jones (1954), vol. I, 128.
136 Ibid., 131.
137 Gay (1988) 12.
138 Lange (1986), table II a, commentary p. 41.
139 STAH, Military Recruitment Board, Muster Roll 1860, D III 6, no. 13.
140 Jones (1954), vol. I, 129.
141 Ibid., 132.
142 Ibid., 120.
143 Ibid.
144 Freud to Martha Bernays, 10 January 1884.
145 Jones (1954), vol. I, 132.
146 Ibid., 74–5.
147 The village of Wandsbek had been upgraded to a town with its own coat of arms in 1870. Since 1937/38 it has belonged to Hamburg, having been incorporated into the city as part of the *Gross-Hamburg-Gesetz* (Greater Hamburg Act). See Kopitzsch and Tilgner (1998) 517.

148 STAH, Genealogical Collection 1. The house no longer exists. In the area where it stood there is now a row of shops and a department store.
149 Schütt (1997) 159.
150 Ibid., 244.
151 Freud to Martha Bernays, 1 December 1885.
152 Jones (1954), vol. I, 147.
153 M. Freud (1957) 42.
154 Sachs (1944) 76.
155 Freud to Martha Bernays, 13 July 1883.
156 Freud to Martha Bernays, 12 August 1885.
157 Jones (1954), vol. I, 133.
158 Ibid., 126. This presumably refers to the hotel 'Zum Alten Posthause' at Schlossstrasse 19/21 (STAH, Hamburg City Directory, 1918/19).
159 Jones (1954), vol. I, 126.
160 Ibid.
161 Ibid., 143.
162 Freud to Martha Bernays, 26 July 1884, cited ibid.
163 Freud to Martha Bernays, 19 October 1885.
164 Gay (1988) 38.
165 Jones (1954), vol. I, 155.
166 Ibid., 155–6.
167 Salber (1999) 38.
168 Gay (1988) 34.
169 Ibid., 37.
170 The 'Rat Man', the lawyer Ernst Lanzer, was one of Freud's 'favourite patients' (Gay (1988) 129). The treatment of the twenty-nine-year-old Lanzer began in 1907, and within just under a year his symptoms – he suffered from obsessional neurosis – had disappeared. The case was regarded as exemplary, providing a model explanation for obsessional neuroses as Freud understood them at the time (see ibid., 261).
171 Freud to Martha Bernays, 21 April 1884.
172 Gay (1988) 44.
173 Ibid.
174 Ibid., 45.
175 Schur (1972) 156.
176 Gay (1988) 43.
177 Freud to Josef Meller, 8 November 1934.
178 Jones (1954), vol. I, 83.
179 Freud to Martha Bernays, 19 October 1885.
180 See Didi-Huberman (2003).
181 Sarah Bernhardt (1844–1923) was an internationally renowned French actress, who achieved fame through her interpretation of *La Dame aux camélias* by Dumas *fils*. With her son Maurice she ran

several theatres in Paris, played classical and modern parts, including male roles, and wrote comedies, novels and memoirs. Freud was a great admirer of the woman and actress Sarah Bernhardt.

182 Julius, born in 1862, was the son of Louis Bernays, who in 1882 had applied to relinquish his German nationality in order to move to Paris with his wife and children (STAH, Genealogical Collection 1).
183 Freud to Martha Bernays, 17 January 1886.
184 Freud to Martha Bernays, 26 November 1885, cited in Appignanesi and Forrester (1992) 27.
185 Jones (1954), vol. I, 148.
186 Gay (1988) 49.
187 Ibid., 50.
188 Freud to Martha Bernays, 20 January 1886.
189 Freud to Martha Bernays, 18 January 1886.
190 Freud to Martha Bernays, 20 January 1886.
191 Freud to Martha Bernays, 2/3 February 1886.
192 Freud to Martha Bernays, 8 March 1886.
193 Jones (1954), vol. I, 156.
194 Ibid., 157.
195 Freud to Martha Bernays, 13 May 1886.
196 Emmeline Bernays to Sigmund Freud, 27 August 1886.
197 Jones (1954), vol. I, 163.
198 See Sigmund Freud (1988). Only a small part of the *Brautbriefe* has so far been published.
199 Jones (1954), vol. I, 109.
200 Salber (1999) 35.
201 Freud to Martha Bernays, 23 June 1882, cited in Jones (1954), vol. I, 122.
202 Freud to Martha Bernays, 30 June 1883, cited ibid., 140.
203 Jones (1954), vol. I, 140.
204 Freud to Martha Bernays, 9 September 1883.
205 Jones (1954), vol. I, 121.
206 Freud to Martha Bernays, 14 August 1882, cited in Appignanesi and Forrester (1992) 30.
207 Freud to Martha Bernays, 14 July 1882, cited ibid.
208 Jones (1954), vol. I, 109.
209 Freud to Martha Bernays, 10 January 1884.
210 Nitzschke (1996) 101.
211 Jones (1954), vol. I, 152.
212 Ibid., 150.
213 Ibid.
214 Ibid., 151.
215 Ibid.
216 Ibid.

217 Ibid., 151–2.
218 Ibid., 129.
219 Ibid., 128.
220 Ibid., 129–30.
221 Ibid., 130.
222 Ibid.
223 See J. Bernays-Heller (1956). Judith Bernays-Heller (1885–1922) was the daughter of Eli Bernays and Anna Freud.
224 Jones (1954), vol. I, 132. Edward Bernays (1891–1995) wrote advertising history when he was called to give a character reference for the opera singer Enrico Caruso in New York in 1920. When the court asked him what his profession was, he answered, 'counsel on public relations', and as such he is regarded as virtually the inventor of the PR adviser as a profession. In the course of a long and illustrious career, in 1923 he wrote *Crystallizing Public Opinion*, even today considered a standard work in the field, and came up with some spectacular ideas for the US advertising market. He received several honorary doctorates and was active in his profession to a ripe old age. He was 103 when he died. See *Der Spiegel* no. 12, 20 March 1995.
225 A. Freud-Bernays (1940).
226 Marriage register of Wandsbek Register Office 1886, no. 81.
227 Schütt (1997) 301.
228 See Loewenthal (1998) 133.
229 Jones (1954), vol. I, 164–5.
230 Gay (1988) 38.
231 Freud to Martha Bernays, 13 July 1883.
232 Jones (1954), vol. I, 128.
233 See Loewenthal (1998) 109. The lighting of the Sabbath lights recalled the creation of light as a divine gift.
234 Sigmund and Martha Freud to Emmeline Bernays, 15 September 1886, cited in Jones (1954), vol. I, 165.
235 Freud to Martha Bernays, 1 April 1884, cited ibid., 154.
236 J. Bernays-Heller (1956).
237 Appignanesi and Forrester (1992) 37.
238 Jones (1954), vol. I, 170.
239 Ibid., 122.
240 Ibid., 166.

PART II   VIENNA

1 Freud to Martha Bernays, 18 August 1882.
2 Clark (1980) 112.

3 Gay (1988) 103. Martha reported that the analysis couch, which Freud later took with him to London, had been given him by his patient Madame Benvenisti around 1890.
4 P. Gay, 'Sigmund and Minna? The Biographer as Voyeur', in *The New York Times Book Review*, 29 January 1989, p. 44, cited in Appignanesi and Forrester (1992) 43.
5 Appignanesi and Forrester (1992) 42.
6 Young-Bruehl (1989) 312.
7 Oskar Pfister to Martha Freud, 12 December 1939, cited in Appignanesi and Forrester (1992) 29.
8 Freud to Anna Freud, 12 October 1920, cited ibid., 43.
9 Gay (1988) 157.
10 Ibid., 158.
11 Ibid., 157.
12 A. W. Freud (1996).
13 Sophie Freud (1995).
14 M. Freud (1957), 11.
15 Freud to Wilhelm Fliess, 16 May 1897.
16 Gay (1988) 169.
17 See Freud to Martha Bernays, 8 November 1886.
18 Gay (1988) 14.
19 W. E. Freud (1987).
20 M. Freud (1957) 38.
21 Berthelsen (1987) 29.
22 Ibid., 27.
23 Ibid.
24 Ibid., 50.
25 M. Freud (1957) 33.
26 See Sophie Freud (1988).
27 Gay (1988) 76.
28 Freud to Max Halberstadt, 7 July 1912.
29 Young-Bruehl (1989) 32.
30 Freud to Martha Bernays, 27 December 1883, cited in Jones (1954), vol. I, 129.
31 Young-Bruehl (1989) 30–1.
32 M. Freud (1957) 14.
33 Young-Bruehl (1989) 32.
34 Ibid.
35 M. Freud (1957) 11.
36 See Roazen (1995) 208.
37 See Roazen (1993) 139.
38 Jones (1954), vol. I, 168.
39 Kollbrunner (2001) 189.
40 Jones (1954), vol. I, 180–1.

41 Daniels (1961).
42 See Gay (1988).
43 Berthelsen (1987) 41.
44 Jones (1957), vol. III, 103.
45 Martha Freud to Paula Fichtl, 25 February 1941.
46 Roazen (1993) 149.
47 Appignanesi and Forrester (1992) 42.
48 Jones (1954), vol. I, 109.
49 Ibid., 153.
50 Ibid., 165.
51 Gay (1988) 40.
52 Jones (1954), vol. I, 134.
53 Ibid., 138.
54 Freud to Martha Bernays, 27 January 1886.
55 Ibid.
56 See Kollbrunner (2001).
57 Freud to Martha Bernays, 16 January 1884.
58 Appignanesi and Forrester (1992) 44.
59 Ibid.
60 Jones (1954), vol. I, 134.
61 Ibid., 114.
62 Roazen (1993) 138.
63 Sigmund Freud to Mathilde Freud, 19 March 1908.
64 See Sigmund Freud (1992) xx. Michael Molnar has compiled a list of the people that appear in Freud's notes between 1929 and 1939 and how often they do so. Freud's daughter Anna heads the list, followed by the other members of the family, the oral surgeon Professor Hans Pichler, Max Eitingon, who was Freud's first training analysand (Gay (1988) 179), and Marie Bonaparte.
65 Clark (1980) 305.
66 The film shot on this occasion is part of a film shown on permanent display in the Freud Museum, with commentary by Anna Freud (home movie).
67 Freud to Max Halberstadt, 27 July 1912.
68 Sigmund Freud to Mathilde Freud, 19 March 1908.
69 Quoted in Gay (1988) 613.
70 Freud to Martha Bernays, 15 November 1883.
71 Freud to Martha Bernays, 25 September 1882.
72 Freud to Martha Bernays, 19 March 1886.
73 See Tögel (1989) and Sigmund Freud (2002).
74 Tögel (1989) 149ff.
75 Freud to Wilhelm Fliess, 23 August 1894.
76 M. Freud (1957) 134.
77 Freud to Lou Andreas-Salomé, 27 July 1916.

78 Roazen (1975) 56.
79 Freud to Wilhelm Fliess, 16 June 1899.
80 Freud to Wilhelm Fliess, 8 July 1899.
81 Freud to Wilhelm Fliess, 16 January 1899.
82 M. Freud (1957) 44.
83 Ibid.
84 Ibid., 59–60.
85 Freud to Wilhelm Fliess, 20 August 1893.
86 M. Freud (1957) 93–4.
87 Ibid., 59.
88 Ibid., 60.
89 Jones (1954), vol. I, 366.
90 See Tögel (1989).
91 Freud to Wilhelm Fliess, 8 August 1897. Masson translates *Unwohlsein* as 'period'.
92 Jones (1954), vol. I, 369.
93 Tögel (1989) 63.
94 Freud to Martha Freud, 15 September 1910.
95 Jones (1954), vol. I, 365.
96 Minna Bernays to Martha Freud, 7 August 1898, cited in Sigmund Freud (2002) 101.
97 Jones (1954), vol. I, 369.
98 See Tögel (1989).
99 Freud to Wilhelm Fliess, 23 October 1898.
100 Freud to Wilhelm Fliess, 23 March 1900.
101 Freud to Wilhelm Fliess, 19 September 1901.
102 Gay (1988) 172.
103 See Sigmund Freud (2002).
104 Gay (1988) 138.
105 Ibid., 136.
106 Sigmund Freud (1992) 73.
107 Freud to his family, 14 June 1930.
108 Freud to Martha Bernays, 12 August 1885.
109 Jones (1954), vol. I, 367.
110 Freud to Wilhelm Fliess, 12 June 1900.
111 Freud to Wilhelm Fliess, 1 February 1900.
112 Gay (1988) 35.
113 Freud to Martha Bernays, 8 March 1886.
114 Freud to Martha Bernays, 30 March 1886.
115 Gay (1988) 180. Freud regarded Karl Abraham (1877–1925) as one of his most gifted adherents. When Abraham died at the age of 48, Freud was so upset at the loss that it was weeks before he could write a letter of condolence to his widow. What was special about Abraham was the precision with which he observed his patients. He is said to

have treated more 'genuine' patients than Freud. (See Eva Jaeggi, 'Schüler und Wegweiser. Der Psychoanalytiker Karl Abraham', in *Die Welt*, 30 Oct. 1999, 9.)

116 The estate in question was formerly the country seat and hunting lodge of the Elector Joachim II. Located in the Reinickendorf district of Berlin, Schloss Tegel in 1765 became the property of the von Humboldt family, for which reason it also bears the nickname *Humboldtschlösschen* (Little Humboldt Castle). Today it is a museum. The psychoanalytical sanatorium was not situated in the castle itself, but in a separate building constructed next to it in 1890 (Ulrich von Heinz (2002) personal communication).

117 Brecht, Friedrich et al. (1992).
118 Ibid.
119 Sigmund Freud (1992) 69.
120 Ibid., 61.
121 Gay (1988) 181.
122 Freud to Karl Abraham, 29 May 1908, cited ibid.
123 Sigmund Freud (1992) 74.
124 Ibid., 140.
125 Young-Bruehl (1989) 124.
126 Anna Freud to Lou Andreas-Salomé, 20 February 1929.
127 Young-Bruehl (1989) 124.
128 Sigmund Freud (1992) 63.
129 Ibid., 66. The entry does not reveal what it was that took Martha to Prague or who it was that she was visiting there.
130 Ibid., 63.
131 Freud to Martha Freud, 1 April 1930, cited ibid.
132 Ibid., 66.
133 Freud to Martha Freud, 9 April 1930, cited ibid.
134 Freud to Ernst Freud, 13 April 1930, cited ibid.
135 Ibid., 123.
136 Ibid., 124.
137 Ibid., 125.
138 Freud to Jeanne Lampl-de Groot, 24 April 1932, cited ibid.
139 Clark (1980) 483.
140 M. Freud (1957).
141 Gay (1988) 173–4. Freud wanted to assemble a number of younger physicians with the 'declared intention of learning, practising and disseminating psychoanalysis'. These followers served Freud as a sort of replacement for Wilhelm Fliess – with whom Freud had by now broken off all contact – and also provided some of the encouragement for which he had been hoping following the publication of his *The Interpretation of Dreams*.
142 Clark (1980) 217.

143 Jones (1954), vol. I, 142.

144 This moral leniency was not something that Martha always displayed. She never forgave Stefan Zweig, a friend of the family, for leaving his wife for a younger woman. Her sympathy went to the woman who had been abandoned, while for Zweig she felt nothing but animosity, a feeling that persisted even when he was in a very bad way himself (see Appignanesi and Forrester (1992) 45–6).

145 Freud to Martha Bernays, 5 July 1885.

146 Roazen (1975) 56.

147 Ibid., 48.

148 A. W. Freud (2001).

149 Roazen (1975) 56.

150 Karl Abraham to Max Eitingon, 1 January 1908, cited in Gay (1988) 158.

151 Gay (1988) 158.

152 M. Freud (1957) 33.

153 Gay (1988) 188.

154 Sigmund Freud (1992).

155 Gay (1988) 191.

156 Eugénie, Princess of Greece and Denmark (1910–89), and Dominique (Dominik), Prince Radziwill (1911–76).

157 Sigmund Freud (1992) 223.

158 Ibid., 49.

159 Jones (1955), vol. II, 203. Rilke was at the time staying in Vienna for military training and was corresponding with Freud. Anna was an out-and-out Rilke enthusiast.

160 Sigmund Freud (1992) 122.

161 Freud to Max Eitingon, 20 March 1932.

162 Hülsemann (1998) 262.

163 See Welsch and Wiesner (1998). There is an opera *Lou Salomé*, written in 1981 by Giuseppe Sinopoli (1946–2001), composer, conductor, archaeologist and a doctor well versed in psychoanalysis, which focuses on the anxiety sexuality implies for Lou Andreas-Salomé. 'Would that I could give you love!' she sings in the libretto (suite no. 1). She is surrounded by men consumed by passion for her, yet she experiences their desire as an insult, indeed as a form of violence. Sigmund Freud is (fictitiously) given the role of releasing her from the obsession of sexuality by making her aware that this is a mental or spiritual, i.e. non-physical, problem.

164 Welsch and Wiesner (1998) 344.

165 See Rothe and Weber (2001). The correspondence between the young Anna and Lou Andreas-Salomé, more than thirty years her senior, was as intensive as it was voluminous, comprising more than 400 letters

over the course of two decades. It soon broke off after Anna had met Dorothy Burlingham.

166 Young-Bruehl (1989) 111–12.
167 Ibid., 113.
168 Ibid., 234.
169 Freud to Sándor Ferenczi, 18 October 1925.
170 Gay (1988) 541.
171 See Bertin (1982).
172 Ibid.
173 Gay (1988) 542.
174 Bertin (1982). It was Martha who brought the topic up, in autumn 1928, apparently without any bidding from Marie.
175 Marie Bonaparte to Freud, 6 September 1937.
176 Henri de Toulouse-Lautrec (1864–1901) came from a family of ancient French aristocracy. Handicapped by a congenital bone disease and two broken legs, he turned to art and from 1884 lived in Montmartre in Paris.
177 Sigmund Freud (1992) 47.
178 Ibid., 62.
179 Ibid., 47.
180 The name of Louis C. Tiffany (1848–1933), who made his mark as a painter, photographer, interior decorator, jewellery designer and ceramicist, is synonymous with lampshades and windows made from stained-glass mosaics, using forms frequently taken from the plant world. His motto was: 'Nature is always right. Nature is beautiful.' He was also inspired by Toulouse-Lautrec.
181 Sigmund Freud (1992) 64.
182 Ibid., 67.
183 Ibid., 128.
184 Young-Bruehl (1989) 137.
185 Appignanesi and Forrester (1992) 81.
186 Josef Breuer (1842–1925), a recognized internist and researcher in experimental physiology, met Freud in Brücke's Institute.
187 See Duda (1992).
188 See Appignanesi and Forrester (1992) 78–80.
189 Freud to Martha Bernays, 13 July 1883.
190 Appignanesi and Forrester (1992) 82.
191 W. E. Freud (1987).
192 Freud to Wilhelm Fliess, 8 November 1895.
193 Freud to Emmeline and Minna Bernays, 16 October 1887.
194 Freud to Wilhelm Fliess, 8 December 1895.
195 See Harsch (2001) 365.
196 Rabadán de Ayala (1998).
197 Gay (1988) 160.

198 Freud to Wilhelm Fliess, 15 July 1896.
199 See Kaplan (1995).
200 M. Freud (1957) 26.
201 Young-Bruehl (1989) 99.
202 Sigmund Freud (1992) 61.
203 M. Freud (1957) 141–2.
204 Freud to Wilhelm Fliess, 8 February 1897.
205 Young-Bruehl (1989) 38.
206 Ibid.
207 M. Freud (1957) 38.
208 Roazen (1993) 44.
209 Roazen (1975) 58.
210 Roazen (1993) 173.
211 Freud to Wilhelm Fliess, 7 March 1896.
212 See Roazen (1993) 165.
213 See Rank (1932).
214 See Reimer, Eckert et al. (1996) 347ff.
215 See Bankl (1999) 195–214. In his youth Freud suffered from various functional and neurotic (psychosomatic) disorders, such as digestive trouble, migraine, rheumatic pains, fear of travelling.
216 M. Freud (1957) 30.
217 Gay (1988) 161.
218 Kollbrunner (2001) 188. Kollbrunner argues that the family structures were aimed at pleasing first and foremost Freud. Though superficially liberal, permissive and 'soft', the climate was in fact – says Kollbrunner – extremely authoritarian and hardly permitted the children any degree of self-determination.
219 W. E. Freud (1987).
220 Freud to his family, 26 June 1930.
221 Martha Freud to Elsa Reiss, 17 January 1950, cited in Gay (1988) 161.
222 Sophie Freud (1988) 80–1.
223 Young-Bruehl (1989) 193.
224 M. Freud (1957) 29.
225 Ibid., 65.
226 Young-Bruehl (1989) 42.
227 M. Freud (1957) 31.
228 Freud to Wilhelm Fliess, 16 October 1895.
229 M. Freud (1957) 31.
230 Ibid., 102.
231 Gay (1988) 371.
232 Ibid., 381.
233 These were the words his son Martin used to sum up the spirit of the celebrations and media reports marking the hundredth anniversary of Freud's birth in 1956 (M. Freud (1957) 9).

234 Gay (1988) 309.
235 A. W. Freud (1996).
236 Ibid.
237 See Anna Freud's obituary for her sister, *Sigmund Freud House Bulletin* vol. 2, no. 1 (1978), cited in Young-Bruehl (1989) 45.
238 Sophie Freud (1988) 4.
239 Sigmund Freud (1992) 55.
240 Sophie Freud (1988) 3.
241 Sigmund Freud (1992) 55.
242 Freud to Sam Freud, 31 December 1930, cited in Sigmund Freud (1992). Sam (Soloman) Freud (1860–1945) was one of the sons of Emanuel Freud (1833–1914), one of Freud's half-brothers who lived in Manchester, from the first marriage of Freud's father.
243 M. Freud (1957) 157.
244 Ibid., 39.
245 Freud to C. G. Jung, 17 February 1911.
246 Roazen (1993) 163.
247 Ibid., 160. Rumour had it that Martin even had a brief affair with Marie Bonaparte.
248 Ibid., 162.
249 Sigmund Freud (1992) 275.
250 A. W. Freud (1996).
251 A. W. Freud (2001).
252 A. W. Freud (1996).
253 Freud to Max Eitingon, 13 December 1920.
254 Young-Bruehl (1989) 41.
255 Jones (1957), vol. III, 103.
256 Freud to Sándor Ferenczi, 17 April 1923.
257 Freud to Ernst Freud, 9 February 1931.
258 Martha Freud to Lucie Freud, 13 November 1933, cited in Sigmund Freud (1992) 169.
259 Sigmund Freud (1992) 180.
260 Martha Freud to Elsa Reiss, 2 December 1945, cited ibid., 263.
261 Ibid.
262 Ibid.
263 A. W. Freud (1996).
264 Chaim Weizmann (1874–1952) in 1918 founded the Hebrew University of Jerusalem. From 1948 to 1952 he was the first president of the State of Israel.
265 Sigmund Freud (1992) 93.
266 A. W. Freud (1996).
267 Krüsmann (2001) 135–6.
268 Young-Bruehl (1989) 42.
269 Gillis-Carlebach (2000) 15.

270 Young-Bruehl (1989) 92.
271 W. E. Freud (1987).
272 Young-Bruehl (1989) 18.
273 Ibid., 38–9.
274 Ibid., 33–4.
275 Ibid., 54.
276 Ibid., 46.
277 Appignanesi and Forrester (1992) 276.
278 See Roazen (1995) 208.
279 Salber (1999) 107.
280 Roazen (1975) 452.
281 A. W. Freud (1996).
282 Olvedi (1992) 34.
283 See Paton and Llobregat (1989) 138.
284 See Olvedi (1992).
285 Hacker (1987) 187.
286 A. W. Freud (2001).
287 W. E. Freud (1987) 201.
288 A. W. Freud (2001).
289 W. E. Freud (1987).
290 A. W. Freud (1996).
291 See Stephan (2000).
292 Appignanesi and Forrester (1992) 43.
293 Roazen (1993) 128.
294 Roazen (1995) 16.
295 Ibid., 67.
296 Ibid., 130.
297 Ibid., 190.
298 Ibid., 208.
299 Roazen (1993) 150.
300 Roazen (1975) 56.
301 Jones (1954), vol. I, 113–14.
302 W. E. Freud (1987).
303 Ibid.
304 Freud to Max Halberstadt, 27 July 1912.
305 Freud to Martha Bernays, 13 July 1883.
306 Jones (1954), vol. I, 145.
307 Freud to Martha Bernays, 15 June 1886, cited ibid., 160.
308 Freud to Wilhelm Fliess, 13 February 1896.
309 Helene Deutsch, née Rosenbach (1884–1982), enrolled at the University of Vienna in 1907, where she was one of the first women to study medicine. In 1918 she began an analysis with Sigmund Freud and subsequently devoted herself to her psychoanalytic training. Her husband was Freud's doctor.

310 Appignanesi and Forrester (1992) 318.
311 Freud to Anna Freud, 22 July 1921.
312 Sigmund Freud (1992) 77.
313 Ibid., 94.
314 Ibid.
315 Martha Freud to Elsa Reiss, 23 February 1939.
316 Dr Felix Deutsch (1884–1964) was Freud's doctor prior to Max Schur.
317 Jones (1957), vol. III, 95; Gay (1988) 419–20. Hajek seemed unruffled by these complications and the almost fatal outcome of the operation he had performed, and the next day he discharged Freud.

PART III   LONDON

1 Sachs (1944) 21.
2 Berthelsen (1987) 74.
3 Jones (1957), vol. III, 234.
4 Berthelsen (1987) 71.
5 Jones (1957), vol. III, 234.
6 M. Freud (1957) 210.
7 Ibid., 212.
8 Young-Bruehl (1989) 227.
9 See Engelman (1976).
10 See Tögel (1990) 1019ff.
11 Gay (1988) 628.
12 See Pross (2000).
13 Speziale-Bagliacca (2000) 75.
14 Martha Freud to Sigmund Freud's sisters, 22 June 1938, cited in Clark (1980) 515.
15 Clark (1980) 514.
16 Jones (1957), vol. III, 248.
17 Martin and Martha Freud to Lilly Marlé, 22 June 1938.
18 See Wegner (2000) 342.
19 See Lehrke (2002).
20 A. W. Freud (2001) and (2002).
21 Princess Eugénie had introduced the Freuds to her husband, Prince Radziwill, at a dinner shortly before their wedding. This was in April 1938, when the Freuds were still in Vienna (Sigmund Freud (1992) 234).
22 Freud to Max Eitingon, 3 November 1938.
23 Tatiana, Princess Radziwill, Marie's granddaughter, was born on 28 August 1939 in Rouen.
24 See Schur (1972).
25 Lux Freud to Felix Augenfeld, 2 October 1939, cited in Schneider (1999) 83.
26 Zweig (1996) 7.

27 Young-Bruehl (1989) 240.
28 Martha Freud to Paul Federn, 5 November 1939.
29 Martha Freud to Margarethe Rie Nunberg, 29 October 1939, cited in Young-Bruehl (1989) 240.
30 Young-Bruehl (1989) 240.
31 Berthelsen (1987) 100.
32 A. W. Freud (2002).
33 Young-Bruehl (1989) 246–7.
34 Berthelsen (1987) 107.
35 At the end of May they were shipped to the Isle of Man, hitherto a holiday paradise for the English middle classes. At first they stayed at the Imperial Hotel. The conditions at Port Erin were relatively liberal, with more or less normal freedom of movement, and a curfew imposed after nine o'clock. Martha wrote her letters to Paula at Port Erin.
36 Anna Freud to Paula Fichtl, 10 August 1940.
37 Martha Freud to Paula Fichtl, 23 August 1940.
38 Martha Freud to Paula Fichtl, 19 August 1940.
39 Martha Freud to Paula Fichtl, 27 September 1940.
40 Martha Freud to Paula Fichtl, 26 September 1940.
41 Martha Freud to Paula Fichtl, 23 August 1940.
42 Martha Freud to Paula Fichtl, 6 September 1940.
43 Martha Freud to Paula Fichtl, 12 September 1940.
44 Ibid.
45 Martha Freud to Paula Fichtl, 27 September 1940.
46 Martha Freud to Paula Fichtl, 4 October 1940.
47 Martha Freud to Paula Fichtl, 25 February 1941.
48 Young-Bruehl (1989) 279–80.
49 See Tögel (1990).
50 Roazen (1975) 56.
51 Roazen (1993) 166.
52 Young-Bruehl (1989) 308.
53 Ibid., 309.
54 Ibid., 308.
55 Quoted ibid.
56 Appignanesi and Forrester (1992) 43.
57 See Young-Bruehl (1989) 423.
58 Freud to Martha Bernays, 4 August 1882.
59 Young-Bruehl (1989) 309.
60 Ibid., 249, 310.
61 Ibid., 310.
62 Berthelsen (1987) 134.
63 Young-Bruehl (1989) 310.
64 See Young-Bruehl (1989).
65 Ibid., 246.

66 Ibid., 312.
67 Ibid.
68 Ibid., 419.
69 Ibid., 311.
70 Gay (1988) 89.
71 Young-Bruehl (1989) 312.
72 Ibid., 310.
73 Jones (1954), vol. I, 109.
74 M. Freud (1957) 21.
75 Jones (1954), vol. I, 109.
76 Roazen (1993) 148.
77 Young-Bruehl (1989) 311.
78 Cited in Appignanesi and Forrester (1992) 45. René Laforgue (1894–1962), a psychiatrist who helped pave the way for psychoanalysis in France, started a correspondence with Freud in 1923. It was on his recommendation that Marie Bonaparte took up her analysis with Freud.
79 Bertin (1982).
80 Freud to Martha Freud, 4 September 1910, cited in Sigmund Freud (2002) 337.
81 Appignanesi and Forrester (1992) 45.
82 Gay (1988) 17.
83 Oskar Pfister to Martha Freud, 12 December 1939.
84 Freud to Martha Bernays, 13 July 1883.
85 Appignanesi and Forrester (1992) 82.
86 See Gay (1988) 83.
87 Ibid., 38.
88 Roazen (1975) 472.
89 Freud to Martha Bernays, 27 January 1886.
90 Gay (1988) 39.
91 Sigmund Freud (1992).
92 Gay (1988) 61.
93 Freud to Wilhelm Fliess, 7 August 1901.
94 Gay (1988) 55.
95 Ibid., 101.
96 Sigmund Freud (1992) 72.
97 See Schröder and Schröder (1992).
98 Salber (1999) 35.
99 Young-Bruehl (1989) 52.
100 Ibid., 185.
101 Ibid., 187.
102 Ibid., 186.
103 Ibid., 187.
104 See Harsch (2001) 371.

105 Appignanesi and Forrester (1992) 273.
106 Young-Bruehl (1989) 187.
107 Ibid., 330.
108 Appignanesi and Forrester (1992) 292.
109 Gay (1988) 160.
110 See Weber-Kellermann (1998).
111 Anna Freud to Kurt Eissler, 2 July 1973, cited in Young-Bruehl (1989) 30.
112 Appignanesi and Forrester (1992) 45–6.

Bibliography

The text is based largely on Sigmund Freud biographies (by Ernest Jones, Peter Gay and others), articles on special issues (women close to Sigmund Freud, reports by family members and patients), works about people from circles close to Freud (e.g. Marie Bonaparte), editions of the letters and diary entries, as well as archive material, interviews and documentaries. Sources as yet unpublished (letters) could only be partially used. Where possible, quotations from Sigmund Freud's letters in translation are taken from Sigmund Freud (1960) or Sigmund Freud (1984) as appropriate. Where this is not possible, an alternative source is given or the translation is by R. G.

Writings by Sigmund Freud mentioned in the text are taken from the *Standard Edition of the Complete Psychological Works of Sigmund Freud* (see entry) and not separately cited in the bibliography.

Appignanesi, L. and Forrester, J. (1992), *Freud's Women*, London.

Bankl, H. (1999), *Woran sie wirklich starben. Krankheiten und Tod historischer Persönlichkeiten*, rev. edn, Vienna, Munich, Bern.

Bernays-Heller, J. (1956), 'Freud's Mother and Father: A Memoir', *Commentary* vol. 21, no. 5, May.

Berthelsen, D. M. (1987), *Alltag bei Familie Freud. Die Erinnerungen der Paula Fichtl*, Hamburg.

Bertin, C. (1982), *Marie Bonaparte: A Life*, New York.

Böhnisch, T. (1999), *Gattinnen. Die Frauen der Elite*, Münster.

Brecht, K., Friedrich, V., Hermanns, L. M., Kaminer, I. J. and Juelich, D. H. (eds) (1992), *Here Life Goes On in a Most Peculiar Way . . .: Psychoanalysis Before and After 1933*, Hamburg.

Burgess, A. (1983), *The End of the World News: An Entertainment*, New York.

Clark, R. W. (1980), *Freud: The Man and the Cause*, London.

Daniels, K. (1961), *Minna's Story: The Secret Love of Dr. Sigmund Freud*, Santa Fe, NM.

De Chellis-Hill, C. (1993), *Henry James' Midnight Song*, New York.

Didi-Huberman, G. (2003), *Invention of Hysteria: Charcot and the Photographic Iconography of the Salpêtrière*, trans. A. Hartz, Cambridge, MA.

Duda, S. (1992), 'Bertha Pappenheim 1859–1936. Erkundungen zur Geschichte der Hysterie oder "Der Fall Anna O." ', in Duda, S. and Pusch, L. F. (eds), *Wahnsinnsfrauen*, vol. 1, Frankfurt am Main.

Engelman, E. (1976), *Berggasse 19: Sigmund Freud's Home and Offices, Vienna, 1938*, New York.

Flem, L. (2003), *Freud the Man: An Intellectual Biography*, trans. S. Fairfield, New York.

Freud, A. W. (1996), 'Mein Grossvater Sigmund Freud', in Tögel, C. (ed.), *Die Biographen aber sollen sich plagen. Beiträge zum 140. Geburtstag Sigmund Freuds*, Sofia.

Freud, A. W. (2001), 'Über meinen Grossvater' (lecture given on the occasion of the opening of the exhibition 'Sigmund Freud. Stationen eines Lebens'), Uchtspringe Specialist Hospital, 1 June.

Freud, A. W. (2002), personal communication.

Freud, M. (1957), *Glory Reflected: Sigmund Freud – Man and Father*, London.

Freud, Sigmund (1953–64), *The Standard Edition of the Complete Psychological Works of Sigmund Freud*, 24 vols, ed. James Strachey, London.

Freud, Sigmund (1960), *Letters of Sigmund Freud, 1873–1939*, ed. E. L. Freud, trans. T. and J. Stern, New York.

Freud, Sigmund (1984), *The Complete Letters of Sigmund Freud to Wilhelm Fliess: 1887–1904*, trans. J. M. Masson, Cambridge, MA.

Freud, Sigmund (1988), *Brautbriefe. Briefe an Martha Bernays aus den Jahren 1882 bis 1886*, ed. E. L. Freud, Frankfurt am Main.

Freud, Sigmund (1992), *The Diary of Sigmund Freud 1929–39: A Record of the Final Decade*, trans. M. Molnar, New York.

Freud, Sigmund (2002), *Unser Herz zeigt nach dem Süden. Reisebriefe 1895–1923*, ed. C. Tögel with the cooperation of M. Molnar, Berlin.

Freud, Sophie (1988), *My Three Mothers and Other Passions*, New York.

Freud, Sophie (1995), 'Buchbesprechung zu: *The Diary of Sigmund Freud 1929–39*', *Psyche* vol. 49, no. 7, July.

Freud, W. E. (1987), 'Die Freuds und die Burlinghams in der Berggasse. Persönliche Erinnerungen', in Leupold-Löwenthal, H. and Scholz-Strasser, I. (eds), *Sigmund-Freud-Vorlesungen 1970–1988*, Böhlau, Vienna, Cologne.

Freud, W. E. (2000), personal communication.

Freud, W. E. (2003), *Zur Bedeutung der Kontinuität früher Beziehungserfahrungen. Konsequenzen aus der psychoanalytischen Entwicklungspsychologie für die Prophylaxe. Gesammelte Schriften 1965–2000*, Frankfurt am Main.

Freud-Bernays, A. (1940), 'My brother, Sigmund Freud', *American Mercury* 51.

Freud-Bernays, A. (2003), *Eine Wienerin in New York*, ed. C. Tögel, Berlin.

Fromm, E. (1959), *Sigmund Freud's Mission*, New York.

Gay, P. (1988), *Freud: A Life for Our Time*, New York.

Gillis-Carlebach, M. (2000), *Jedes Kind ist mein Einziges. Lotte Carlebach-Preuss. Antlitz einer Mutter und Rabbiner-Frau*, Hamburg.

Gödde, G. (2003), *Mathilde Freud. Die älteste Tochter Sigmund Freuds in Briefen und Selbstzeugnissen*, Giessen.

Hacker, F. (1987), 'Nachwort', in Berthelsen (1987).

Hamburg City Directory (see State Archives of Hamburg).

Harsch, H. E. (2001), 'Zur Geschichte und Psychodynamik der Doppelbemutterung', *Psyche* vol. 55, no. 4, April.

Hülsemann, I. (1998), *Lou: Das Leben der Lou Andreas-Salomé*, Munich.

Jones, E. (1954–7), *Sigmund Freud: Life and Work* (3 vols), London.

Kaplan, M. A. (1995), *The Making of the Jewish Middle Class: Women, Family and Identity in Imperial Germany*, New York and Oxford.

Kollbrunner, J. (2001), *Der Kranke Freud*, Stuttgart.

Kopitzsch, F. and Brietzke, D. (eds) (2001), *Hamburgische Biographie. Personenlexikon*, vol. 1, Hamburg.

Kopitzsch, F. and Tilgner, D. (eds) (1998), *Hamburg-Lexikon*, Hamburg.

Krüll, M. (1979), *Freud and His Father*, trans. A. J. Pomerans, New York.

Krüsmann, E. (2001), 'Mit den Freuds auf der Couch. Interview mit Bella und Esther Freud', *ELLE*, September.

Lange, H. W. (1986), *A Genealogical Study of the Bernays Family. Table I–III*. Freud Museum, London.

Lehrke, G. (2002), *Wie einst Lili Marleen. Das Leben der Lale Andersen*, Berlin.

Loewenthal, E. (1998), *Judentum*, Bern, Munich, Vienna.

Louven, A. (1991a), *Die Juden in Wandsbek*, rev. edn, Hamburg.

Louven, A. (1991b), 'Martha Freud. Ein Lebensbild', in Herzig, A. (ed.), *Die Juden in Hamburg 1590 bis 1990*, Hamburg.

Nitzschke, B. (1996), *Wir und der Tod. Essays über Sigmund Freuds Leben und Werk*, Göttingen.

Olvedi, U. (1992), *Frauen um Freud. Die Pionierinnen der Psychoanalyse*, Freiburg, Basel, Vienna.

Paton, L. and Llobregat, G. (1989), *Freud. Prénom Martha*, Paris.

Pross, S. (2000), *In London treffen wir uns wieder. Vier Spaziergänge durch ein vergessenes Kapitel deutscher Kulturgeschichte*, Berlin.

Rabadán de Ayala, C. (1998), 'Martha Bernays. The unknown face of Freud. A psychoanalytical approach' (lecture given at the conference on *The Role of Women in the History of Psychoanalysis*, International Association for the History of Psychoanalysis, London, July 1998).

Rank, O. (1932), *Art and Artist: Creative Urge and Personality Development*, trans. C. F. Atkinson, New York.

Reimer, C., Eckert, J., Hautzinger, M. and Wilke, E. (1996), *Psychotherapie. Ein Lehrbuch für Ärzte und Psychologen*, Berlin, Heidelberg, New York.

Richard, H. (1993), 'Une vision post-scientifique de la modernité dans la clinique psychanalytique', *Filigrane, Revue de Psychanalyse* vol. 2, no. 1, www.rsmq.com.org/filigrane/archives/vision.htm.

Rieder, I. (1994), *Wer mit Wem. Hundert Jahre lesbische Liebe. Berühmte Frauen, ihre Freundinnen, Liebhaberinnen und Lebensgefährtinnen*, Vienna.

Roazen, P. (1975), *Freud and his Followers*, New York.

Roazen, P. (1993), *Meeting Freud's Family*, Amherst, MA.

Roazen, P. (1995), *How Freud Worked: First-Hand Accounts of Patients*, Northvale, NJ.

Rothe, D. A. and Weber, I. (eds) (2001), *Als käm ich heim zu Vater und Schwester. Lou Andreas-Salomé – Anna Freud. Briefwechsel 1919–1937*, vols. 1 and 2, Göttingen.

Roudinesco, E. and Kapnist, E. (1997), 'Sigmund Freud. L'invention de la psychanalyse', TV documentary film, broadcast on ARTE, 13 October 1998 (part 1) and 14 October 1998 (part 2).

Sachs, H. (1944), *Freud: Master and Friend*, Cambridge, MA.

Salber, W. (1999), *Sigmund und Anna Freud. Duographie*, Hamburg.

Sartre, J.-P. (1985), *The Freud Scenario*, trans. Q. Hoare, Chicago.

Schneider, P. (1999), *Sigmund Freud*, Munich.

Schröder, M. M. and Schröder, M. S. (1992), *Spiegel der Seele. Erleben, was Gestaltende Psychotherapie sein kann*, Stuttgart.

Schur, M. (1972), *Freud: Living and Dying*, London.

Schütt, E. C. (ed.) (1997), *Chronik Hamburg*, rev. edn, Gütersloh, Munich.

Speziale-Bagliacca, R. (2000), *Sigmund Freud. Begründer der Psychoanalyse*, Heidelberg.

State Archives of Hamburg (STAH), Hamburg-Wandsbek. Genealogical Collection 1 (Bernays and Halberstadt). Guardianship Court Files, Commercial Court Files, Supplementary Files, Hamburg City Directory Archives.

Stephan, I. (1992), *Die Gründerinnen der Psychoanalyse. Eine Entmythologisierung Sigmund Freuds in zwölf Frauenportraits*, Stuttgart.

Stephan, I. (2000), *Das Schicksal der begabten Frau im Schatten berühmter Männer*, Stuttgart.

Stone, I. (1971), *The Passions of the Mind: A Biographical Novel of Sigmund Freud*, Garden City, NY.

Theweleit, K. (1994), *Object Choice: All You Need is Love*, trans. M. Green, London.

Tichy, M. and Zwettler-Otte, S. (1999), *Freud in der Presse: Rezeption Sigmund Freuds und der Psychoanalyse in Österreich 1895–1938*, Vienna.

Tögel, C. (1989), *Berggasse – Pompeji und zurück. Sigmund Freuds Reisen in die Vergangenheit*, Tübingen.

Tögel, C. (1990), 'Bahnstation Treblinka. Zum Schicksal von Sigmund Freuds Schwester Rosa Graf', *Psyche* vol. 44, no. 11, November.

Tögel, C. (1996), *Freuds Wien. Eine biographische Skizze nach Schauplätzen*, Vienna.

Tsalikoglou, F. (2000), *I, Martha Freud*, Athens.

Weber-Kellermann, I. (1998), *Frauenleben im 19. Jahrhundert. Empire und Romantik, Biedermeier, Gründerzeit*, Munich.

Wegner, M. (2000), *Ja, in Hamburg bin ich gewesen. Dichter in Hamburg*, Hamburg.

Welsch, U. and Wiesner, M. (1998), *Lou Andreas-Salomé. Vom Lebensurgrund zur Psychoanalyse*, Munich, Vienna.

Wortis, J. (1994), *My Analysis with Freud*, London.

Xenakis, F. (1986), *Zut, on a encore oublié Madame Freud*, Paris.

Young-Bruehl, E. (1989), *Anna Freud: A Biography*, London.

Zweig, A. (1996), *Freundschaft mit Freud. Ein Bericht*, Berlin.

Index